# THE CULTURAL CREATION

# OF

# CHRISTIANITY

Howard M. Snider, Ph.D.

Copyright © 2005 by Howard M. Snider

ISBN  0-7414-2370-7


Photography and Design by Vada Snider.


*Published by:*

**INFINITY**
PUBLISHING.COM

*1094 New De Haven Street, Suite 100*
*West Conshohocken, PA 19428-2713*
*Info@buybooksontheweb.com*
*www.buybooksontheweb.com*
*Toll-free  (877) BUY BOOK*
*Local Phone (610) 941-9999*
*Fax  (610) 941-9959*

*Printed in the United States of America*

*Printed on Recycled Paper*

*Published  January 2005*

# TABLE OF CONTENTS

*Jewish, Greek and Roman ideas about the supernatural world, and its intrusion into this world, became the framework used by early church theologians in their effort to explain and understand Jesus.*

## Section C
## Gradual change through a millennium, then rapid change under the influence of Martin Luther and John Calvin

*The confluence of the enlightenment, scientific thought and social discontent produced, among other things, the protestant reformation. Subsequent denominational fragmentation laid the foundations for religious individualism and modern-day Christian fundamentalism.*

## Section D
## Contemporary types of Christianity

*Contemporary types of Christianity fall along a continuum, bounded by two extremes. One extreme, Constantinian Christianity, reflects the early creeds and derivative ideas. The other emphasizes Jesus' ethical teachings.*

*In spite of dogmas and doctrines antithetical to Jesus' purposes and teachings, a thin thread of Jesus' work persists among 21st-century Christians.*

# APPENDICES

# A PERSONAL NOTE FROM THE AUTHOR

I am a member of the Mennonite Church, a small denomination in the tradition of the Anabaptist movement, which developed during the reformation of the 16th century. This denomination is sometimes defined as neither Protestant, Catholic nor Jew.[1]

I have been thinking about religion, and particularly the Christian religion since the earliest Sunday School days. By the age of 7 or 8, two problems engaged my mind: "Where did God come from?" and "Why is there anything?" Now, after more than 75 years, I think I have found an answer to the first question.

Through the years, other religious questions have also required thought. The Jesus of 30 CE (Common Era) and the Jesus of Constantinian Christianity seem to be antithetical. The question then is "How did Jesus, the story-telling ethicist, turn into the Jesus of the creeds?"

Since my youth I have engaged, at first hand, a variety of Christian denominations: various branches of the Mennonite Church, United Church of Canada, Evangelical Free Church, Christian and Missionary Alliance Church, and the Western Canadian Bible Institute in Regina, Saskatchewan. All implicitly or explicitly, and in varying degrees, affirm the imponderables of the traditional Christian creeds and confessions. Most provide no rational resolution to the recurring conundrums and mysteries of creedal and doctrinal statements.

My seminary experiences, terminating in a bachelor of divinity degree in 1957, suggested that Jesus of the first century had significance for life – even life in the 20th century. I began to sense this Jesus was remarkably unlike the Jesus of the fourth-century creeds and many modern-day confessions of faith.

Throughout my adult life I have been constantly engaged in research, reflection and writing relative to the contradictions between the ethical teachings of Jesus and the mystical creedal pronouncements of much of western Christianity. Other activities in my life during these years include a period of ministry at the Holyrood Mennonite Church in Edmonton, Alberta; completion of a master's degree at the University of Alberta and a doctorate at the University of Kansas; and more than 25 years as Professor of Sociology at Bethel College, North Newton, Kansas.

This book is a sampling of some reflections and conclusions about these religious matters, which are meaningful for me. I hope, by reading them, you will be motivated to think more meaningfully about your own beliefs.

*Howard M. Snider, Ph.D.*

# CREDITS

The material in this book is a product of more than 70 years of personal struggle to understand the Bible and its relationship to various expressions of Christianity. The people who helped me are innumerable. Some of you will recognize your own ideas. Please accept my thanks.

A special thanks to the "Edmonton group" whose openness, curiosity, creativity and courage provided the context for some of the most exhilarating days of my life. This book, in many ways, is an outcome of those exciting days nearly 50 years ago.

One can read many books in 80 years. Again the sources are innumerable. I have deliberately not burdened the copy with references and sources. I started this project to clarify issues for myself. References and allusions can be checked by easy searches. I invite you to get involved with the ideas and expand them.

To the innumerable authors, dead and alive, and the multitude of friends who contributed to my thoughts – my heartfelt thanks.

I owe more than I know to a minister in my home church in rural Saskatchewan in my early childhood. Moses Schmidt may not have known the word "ethical" but he preached about "right living." Very rarely was he concerned with the notions of creedal doctrines. I am beginning to realize what a marvelous blessing that was.

# PREFACE

This book is concerned with different kinds of Christianity. It is not a discussion of denominational differences.

What is in view here is a difference at a fundamental level. A difference in an understanding of Jesus' purpose in this world.

Is Jesus to be understood as a way of life or as the central actor in a forensic drama – a supernatural figure in a complex belief system? If there is a difference at this point we are then in the presence of two distinctly different kinds of Christianity. These might be called "Jesus Christianity" and "Constantinian Christianity." Both kinds of Christianity exist, to some degree, in all Christian individuals and denominations. However, although these types of Christianity coexist they are not causally connected.

In a theoretical sense they may be understood as extremes of a continuum and can be described in ideal terms. This is the way they will be treated in this book. Theoretically an individual might be a pure "Jesus Christian." Another might be a pure "Constantinian Christian." Most people will find themselves and their churches somewhere in between.

For the sake of understanding the complex mix of Christian beliefs and behaviors, I have made sharp distinctions between these two kinds of Christianity. I have attempted to develop a model within which Christians might measure their own beliefs and behaviors. I invite you to discover a place for yourself on this continuum.

# EARLY CULTURAL INFLUENCES ON CHRISTIANITY

*As Christianity developed in the first four centuries CE, key characteristics of Jewish, Greek and Roman cultures became core characteristics of Christianity. As a result of these many influences, Jesus' original ethical message is a very small thread in modern Christianity.*

| CULTURAL CHARACTERISTICS | CHARACTERISTICS OF CHRISTIANITY |
|---|---|

## JEWISH CULTURE

**Prophetic Tradition**
- Ethical messiah/Jesus ⟶ Followers

**Priestly Tradition**
- Political messiah ⟶ Kingdom ideas
- God above all gods ⟶ Monotheism
- Chosen people ⟶ Exclusiveness

## GREEK CULTURE

**Common Theology**
- God-Men ⟶ God-Man
- Mystery religions ⟶ Blood sacrifices / Purification
- View of the future ⟶ Resurrection / Union with the gods

## ROMAN CULTURE

**Religion**
- Contract relationships ⟶ Services / Bond rituals

**Social Classes**
- Emperor ⟶ Pope
- Senators ⟶ Cardinals
- Officials ⟶ Priests
- Commoners ⟶ Parishioners

**Administration**
- Hierarchical organization ⟶ Hierarchical / Rigid society

**Military**
- Authority and techniques ⟶ Obedience / Fear / Coercion

# CHAPTER 1

# THE SOCIAL WORLD OF JESUS

It is a common assumption that Jesus was the founder of Christianity. The New Testament of the Bible, in a most uncritical reading, would seem to support such a contention.

An elemental understanding of contemporary Christianity suggests an unbroken line from the historical Jesus to the "Christ" of Paul and the "Christ" of the New Testament. It seems the early church fathers assumed a similar continuity into their creeds and doctrines.

Twentieth century American religious fundamentalists likewise assume a direct connection between Jesus, the portrayal of Jesus in the New Testament, the Jesus Christ of the fourth and fifth century creeds, the Anselmic formulations of the 11th century and their own theological dogmas.

But serious study of the work of Jesus in his social context compared with these dogmas and contemporary representations of Christianity suggest startling contradictions.

A superficial understanding of Christian history suggests Jesus and Christianity were central features and dominant social realities of Palestine and the Middle East in the first century. Nothing could be further from the truth. Jesus and Christianity were in fact exceedingly minor players in

Palestine of the time. They merit no more then a few sentences by historians of the period and Christians numbered no more than a few thousand by the beginning of the second century.

If they influenced the world of their day it was a miniscule impact compared to the way they were influenced by the cultures in which they lived. The Christianity which emerged from these interactions was an amalgam of local cultural beliefs and practices, tempered in some ways by ideas and spiritual elements they had come to associate with Jesus.

Let us begin with the observation: Jesus was not a Christian. This is a biblical position since the term "Christian" did not appear until many years after the death of Jesus.[2]

Palestine in the first century of the Common Era (CE) was a dynamic social world. It was a region of many interacting peoples. Palestine was populated by diverse groups. It was an amalgam of many cultures regionally differentiated and ever changing. The inhabitants could not escape the many and diverse cultural strains. This is the kind of world in which Jesus and his followers lived. If we are to understand Jesus, his message and his followers we must understand their world.

It was a changing social world. Palestine was indeed something of a melting pot. It was on a major trade route for centuries and such commerce left cultural traces of many kinds. Neither Jesus nor Christianity developed independently of numerous currents of thought. Like all peoples and their institutions, Jesus and Christianity were and are products of a real social world.

At the core of this cultural mix were many currents, but three are most evident.

The dominant cultural strain was Hellenistic, a legacy of the conquests of Alexander the Great and the subsequent diffusion of Greek culture throughout the entire Middle East. Although elements of classical Greek thought were still present in intellectual circles, it was the variety of mystery religions of Asia Minor and the Near East which informed the weltanschauung of the polyglot populations of the region. No one living in the area could escape these influences.

A second basic current was Roman culture. Rome dominated the Near East militarily and politically for many decades and its institutional forms and cultural life were inescapable. By the third century the Christian church had expanded into the western Roman world where its theology and organization became relatively fixed.

A third current was the heritage imbedded in a minority ethnic group descended from the Patriarch Jacob – the Jewish people. This ethnic group was a small portion of the population of the region.

Students of the era generally describe the culture of the region as Greco-Aramaic although individual ethnic groups maintained elements of their traditional religious and community patterns. Certainly remnants of ancestral cultures persisted in their local forms but these were modified as they interacted with one another and overlapped and amalgamated with Greek and Roman culture.

Thus, Palestine and the Near East of the first century was not an enclave of Jews or any other pure and independent culture. The assumption that any of them were successful in maintaining a separate and pure ethnic tradition is patently false.

It was a time of great social ferment. Change is not a modern invention. Judaism was conservative, but so were Roman and Greek cultures. It is the nature of cultures to be conservative, but social change occurs in spite of conserva-

3

tive forces.

These realities may be illustrated by a glance at two communities separated by less than six miles: Nazareth and Sepphoris.[3] Nazareth was a small village with fewer than 20 families. Nazareth, like other neighboring villages, was the residence area of peasants who walked to their fields and orchards. The villagers also occupied themselves with trades and crafts necessary for survival in such an agricultural community.

What there was by way of local activities beyond interfamilial social interaction would be highly speculative. There is no record of a synagogue or any other formal religious organization in the village. The Jewish ethnic characteristics were imbedded in the family's rituals and practices, but these had little relevance to the formal temple and religious functionaries of far-off Jerusalem.

The Jewish culture was compromised of many things, including the Aramaic language. This language, as all languages, had the capacity to modify concepts and perspectives. The villagers of Nazareth, in spite of their Jewish ethnicity, were products of the Greek and Aramaic thought patterns that were pervasive in the area. At least to some extent, Jesus' family and friends saw the world through Greek and Aramaic eyes.

Sepphoris was a much larger town, populated by the descendents of peoples who had been there long before the Jews had arrived, as well as more recent immigrants from all areas of the Near East and the Roman world. It was a polyglot town with a mix of cultures. It was the Roman political center of Galilee. The populace was bilingual, using Greek and Aramaic.

A major rebuilding and expansion of Sepphoris was undertaken by Herod Antipas between 4 BCE and 39 CE –

the period spanning the entire life of Jesus. In this cosmopolitan town, Greco-Roman culture flourished. Its philosophical orientations, institutional structures, religious beliefs, rituals and worship sites were dedicated to Roman, Greek and Syrian deities. A theatre was built during this period.

Recent archeological work indicates the remnants of Gymnasia for sports activities and Stoa for intellectual discussion.

Sepphoris was a thriving town in the time of Jesus, variously estimated at 12,000 to 20,000. For the time and region it was a powerful political and cultural center, yet Sepphoris is not even mentioned in the New Testament. Why did the authors of the gospel accounts avoid reference to this dynamic and influential urban setting within easy walking distance of Jesus' home? And Sepphoris was not the only Greco-Roman town of the region. There were enough such towns in the area to earn it the name Decapolis, meaning "ten towns."

This was the physical and social environment in which Jesus grew to maturity. It beggars the imagination to think that an intelligent, curious, young Jesus and his peers – growing up in Nazareth – were unacquainted with Sepphoris and the life of the surrounding towns.

There is no way in which Jesus could have escaped the effects of the Jewish influences of his home and family social group. Likewise, there is no way he could have escaped the culture of Sepphoris and the non-Jewish peasant villages near by.

This is also the milieu in which early Christianity arose. These are the elements which we must understand if we are to understand Jesus and the emergence of Christianity.

It seems that Jesus' family were practicing Jews, although

we have little information about the religious activity of his father Joseph. This is a remarkable deficiency in our knowledge of Jesus' early religious life. Jesus was certainly acquainted with the rituals, festivals and family practices of Judaism of his day. He apparently had some contact with official priestly dimensions of Judaism, but the results were unpleasant and ultimately disastrous for his life and work.

As an intelligent and curious child and teenager, Jesus' world was certainly much larger than religion, just as it is for every human being. And what of Jesus' social group? Surely there were friends of the family, but also peer friends and acquaintances both male and female. Moreover, it is impossible to believe that Jesus was ignorant of the people in Sepphoris and the multitude of non-Jewish neighbors. An immaculate ethnic intellectual environment is an impossibility.

One remarkable feature of Jewish culture was the affinity for discussion, argument and debate. This mode of socializing was integral to Jewish culture. Although the formal discussion by the elders may have emphasized religious topics, there was much more to life than religion. Given such a cultural context, one must entertain the possibility of intense conversation about a wide range of topics among adolescents, young people and young adults in the village. One does a lot of thinking, talking and changing up to the age of 27. Can one imagine Jesus to be an exception? One might be confident these discussions ranged widely and occurred at levels of intensity and depth foreign to our TV-cursed generation.

Although literacy levels were low and books rare, there was access to Jewish, Greek and Roman oral literature. There was a vast reservoir of sayings and stories, from many sources and of many genres. The retelling of these stories and aphorisms informed and shaped life. It is the way all peoples transmit culture, inculcate folkways and moral standards, and accomplish informal social control.

The wisdom literature circulating in Palestine in the first century was hardly a new creation. Ideas have a way of sifting through the barriers of culture and are fluid enough to move along the paths of commerce. The content of this literature was the legacy of the Far East and the Near East. The stories, parables and wise sayings circulating in the complex mix of cultures in Palestine were hardly original with anyone – including Jesus.

This wisdom literature reflected elements of the dominant cultures of the region, but also included elements of ancient Zoroastrianism, Judaism, and even notions that lie at the core of ancient Chinese and Indian thought. Most obvious, surely, is the common-sense wisdom of many peoples as they explained life and formulated customs that made social life possible in communities. Many of these were universal – the common property of many cultures. Some were unique to specific circumstances and specific communities.

The canonical materials have no reference to Jesus writing. We have nothing from his hand. We have only wise sayings and stories purportedly from his mouth. Given the literary standards of the day we can have no certainty about either the authorship or accuracy of the reported activities or stories. Jesus lived in a dynamic social world in which the modification and reformulation of wise and practical teachings was practiced.

Jesus tapped this vast reservoir of common knowledge and made this wisdom literature his own. The gospels, including the non-canonical writings, demonstrate the range of materials familiar to Jesus. Moreover, he had the courage to refurbish and cast stories and aphorisms into unique settings with startling implications. He communicated the ancient and current wisdom in ways that made people listen.

Jesus is portrayed as a remarkable teacher; a teacher in some unique way inseparable from the moral and ethical implications of his messages. He is portrayed as one who loves, cares and forgives without end. He is portrayed as one who meets violence with the redemptive power of love. He is portrayed as the very incarnation of his teachings; a singular accomplishment.

Obviously he was more than a repository of wise sayings. He was a remarkable person, a superior human being. In the language of our day, we might describe Jesus as a highly evolved social being. A true and complete human being. A fully developed human being.

The authors of the gospels succeeded in capturing this quality of Jesus. His followers have bound him to a rich body of wisdom literature and thus enabled him to be the founder of a remarkable and enduring ethical social movement.

But these same authors included mystical, magical elements consistent with their native cultures. The meaning of Jesus' life and work has been perverted by these cultural accretions and violent distortions. These additions, entirely foreign to Jesus' message and purpose, ultimately crystallized in a supernatural "Christ." This "Christ" emerged as the dominant and sustaining myth of the church by the third and fourth centuries.

The difference between Jesus and this "Christ" is remarkable. They have little in common. It is astounding that 21st century Christian fundamentalism, preoccupied with a mystical supernatural Christ, has the effrontery to claim Jesus as the founder of its religion. This mystifying connection merits some serious analysis.

Jesus, after his death, was decreasingly an influential factor in the development of a religion which has come to be called

Christianity. By the time of the writing of the four gospels, which appear in the New Testament, the distorting effects of Greek, Roman and Jewish religious thought were already prominent and formative. By the fourth and fifth centuries, little of Jesus' ethical work remained in the teachings of the church. What did remain was cast in the images, symbols and terminology of mystery cults.

If we are to recover the essentials of Jesus' contribution to humanity, we must strip away those elements of the Jewish, Greek and Roman cultures that have corrupted the record of his life, purpose and work. The task ahead is the location and description of the cultural factors which changed the man Jesus – the remarkable teacher and practitioner of an ethical way of life – into the central figure of the sacrificial mystery religion of Creedal, Constantinian, Anselmic and much of modern Christianity.

## CHAPTER 2

# CHRISTIANITY AND THE JEWISH CULTURE

The ancient world was full of supernatural forces and personifications of these forces in deities and spirits of various kinds. Most were related to basic human needs of food, fertility and security. Tribal deities were particularly necessary and important in providing protection when danger threatened from competing social groups or problematic physical events.

Tribal deities tended to be rooted in the soil of a territory. But the God of Abraham, Isaac and Jacob, according to Jewish tradition, was a mobile God who followed this developing and expanding group from the Ur of the Chaldees, to Palestine, to Egypt and back to Palestine.

The Israelites recognized the gods of Egypt and the gods of the peoples they encountered in their treks from one place to another. But their God "Yahweh" developed a number of special characteristics. There was a growing sense that Yahweh was more powerful than the gods of other tribal groups of the region, even more powerful than the gods of Egypt.

Numerous interpretations of the Israelites' history were developed and elaborated. We know these as the stories of the exodus: the plagues, the parting of the waters of the Red Sea, the survival in the desert by the provision of manna, the escape from the scourge of desert beasts, the successful passage through lands of hostile peoples and finally the crossing of the Jordan.

A whole generation perished on this pilgrimage, but their descendents in Palestine finally experienced some security and stability even among alien peoples. In spite of the cultural diversity of their environment, a remarkable sense of tribal unity merged into a sense of nationhood and power. King David and King Solomon were able to exert influence not only among the tribal descendants of Abraham, but also among other tribes of this Semitic world.

These remarkable developments, they concluded, could not have happened without the direct assistance and intervention of the supernatural. Their God Yahweh, they were convinced, had done marvelous things.

At the core of this history lay two remarkable social inventions that the Israelites attributed to Yahweh. One was the organization of the people into tribal groups each with its own internal structure designed to produce and maintain order. Each group had a strong sense of tribal identity, but also an understanding of unity with all the other tribes. The second social invention was the Decalogue, a moral code designed to structure social relationships in the community. Both of these were attributed to Yahweh.

Thus, societal order and ordered relationships between people were made sacred. The way people behaved with one another was a matter of concern to their deity. This was a unique role for a tribal deity. The deities of other peoples in the Near East had no such responsibility.

The trek – with its beginning in the Ur of the Chaldees, the events on the way and the final arrival in Palestine – created a marvelous range of oral material. What did all this mean? And what did their ancestors, Abraham, Isaac and Jacob (whether real or mythical) mean in the context of their societal pilgrimage?

In these respects, the children of Israel were no different than any other ethnic group that ever lived. All peoples, in every generation, struggle with this question. What is the meaning of it all?

The oral stories recounted not only memories of events, but also interpretations of these memories. In the oral processes, the accounts of events and interpretations were modified. Each new telling incorporated elements of current reality. Sharpening occurred, some elements disappeared, accretions appeared. Interpretations changed. Ultimately, these modified stories and interpretations were written by people who had no firsthand information about any of the events.

As the stories became history, the assessments of the gods of the ancestors changed.

Certainly, the descendants of Jacob were aware of multiple deities. The gods of Egypt were powerful, but obviously not powerful enough to prevent the escape of the Israelites. They could only conclude that Yahweh was superior. The same logic was applied to every trial they encountered. Obviously, their God was superior to the gods of all the tribes and lands through which they trekked.

By the time of written history, crucial ancestral tribal events were explained in terms of Yahweh's intervention. In all of this, the character of Yahweh was exhibited. He had rescued them from slavery, subdued all enemies, provided manna and given them a land. Moreover, he formed them into an organized society with a superior moral code. He made them his own special people and revealed himself as a moral God. At least, this was their interpretation of their history.

They came to believe that Yahweh incorporated – in one deity – the power and attributes, which in other tribal groups were distributed among multiple gods. By comparison, all other gods were weak, chaotic, confused, immoral, maybe even frauds.

Yahweh alone, according to their interpretation, was their God. This understanding resulted in a remarkable self-assessment, a conviction of uniqueness, a feeling of being a chosen people. In their own assessment, the Israelites were a special people, a special power, a special kingdom and a special national group. They were also a people with a special morality and a special mission in this world.

For them, Yahweh became the superior God of the universe – maybe the only God. Monotheism was born. Any other people who talked about their gods were considered devotees of weak and immoral gods, or dupes of false gods.

But there was much more. Being Yahweh's chosen people imposed a great responsibility. They were called to demonstrate the superior qualities of Yahweh in a national state. In addition, they had a divine mission to share the message of monotheism and the sacred moral code.

In the changing fortunes of their political and social life, a few events affirmed these ideologies. But other events quickly and oppressively called into question the ideology of superiority and separateness. The power of the Jewish state was short-lived and the moral superiority of the tribes and the people was increasingly hard to prove.

As the centuries passed, two divergent views of their purpose in the world developed.

At one extreme was the conviction that God had called them to be a nation, a political entity separate from other societies, with a significant destiny. A hope for the restoration of an idealized kingdom of David and Solomon emerged. This expectation characterized the priestly tradition.

At the other extreme was an emphasis on the moral dimensions of their unique encounter with the monotheistic power of the universe. This gave rise to efforts designed to restore the nation and community to the pristine moral and ethical dimensions which some had come to associate with Yahweh. The prophetic tradition was born.

Between these extremes were various amalgams. The discussions and debates in the synagogues and other social groups in Palestine and Diaspora must have been intense.

Certainly not all was well. The kingdom was gone. Subjugation to alien and polytheistic societies occurred many times. Their status as a subject and dependent people without a real state and without meaningful power was pure proof that Yahweh's expectations for them had not been realized. Even the Maccabean revolutionary attempt led nowhere.

It became clear that a renewed intervention of Yahweh was the only way to return to the good old days. The days when they were first chosen by Yahweh and experienced the glorious state and nation under King David and King Solomon. Surely the monotheistic God who had selected them as his special people would not betray his own choice. He would send his messenger, the Messiah, who would reestablish the kingdom and be something of a reincarnation of King David.

In addition, all was not well with the moral and ethical dimensions of Jewish society. People were entranced by the gods of neighboring tribes. Moral decay was evident. They were not much different than the surrounding ethnic groups.

The moral and ethical life to which Yahweh had called them was in taters.

For many, this condition was unbearable. Surely the monotheistic God who had called them to be representatives of morality in the world would not give up his moral plan for all people. They had failed. But Yahweh was faithful. He would intervene. He would act by sending a messenger, the Messiah, who would establish a moral society and inspire people to live morally and responsibly.

With this range of understandings, the concept of the Messiah was confused and fluid. The myth of the Messiah, in Jewish society, varied from time to time, place to place and from one social group to another.

Some expected the Messiah to be a political, maybe even a military figure. Certainly under such divine intervention their power among nations would be restored. They would again take their place among respected and feared nations of the world, never again subject to foreign kings.

Others expected the Messiah to lead a renewal in a spiritual domain. The renewed Jewish state would be a moral power, a nation whose character would enlighten the dark world. They, as the people of the monotheistic God, would expose the false and fabricated gods of surrounding peoples. As the shining light of the only true God, the Jews would lead all people to rise above their idols and worship the only real God of the universe.

Others were not so certain of this national calling. They looked at the conditions of their society and communities and saw envy, bitterness, strife, poverty, rivalry, injustice, other moral and ethical failures; and felt the pain of such social conditions. Some had no confidence in a literal application of the supernatural Messianic myth and they struggled to make interpretations useful for everyday life.

For these people, the Messiah embodied the moral and ethical dimensions of Yahweh as these could be lived and expressed in the everyday realities of human relationship.

In this latter perspective, there were two radical departures from the nationalistic ideology. One was the complete rejection of the sacrificial rituals and religious ceremonies so central to the priestly tradition. Amos, an advocate of this view known as the prophetic tradition, asked the question, "With what shall I come before the Lord and bow myself before God on high? Shall I come before him with burnt offerings, with calves of a year old? Will the Lord be pleased with thousands of rams and ten thousand rivers of oil? Shall I give my first born for my transgression, the fruit of my body for the sin of my soul?."[4] The answer is a profound and resounding NO! Sacrifice as a way of serving God is out and, even more clearly, sacrifice as a solution for sin is forever rejected in the prophetic tradition.

But the Amos and Micah tradition has an additional dramatic message. "He has showed you, oh man, what is good and what does the Lord require of you but to do justice, and to love kindness and to walk humbly with your God."[5]

The people of God, according to these prophetic materials, are those people who reject exclusive status and all forms of sacrifice. All the notions of being a special people, in a special land, with a special political destiny are wiped away. What is left is a special quality of life. The people of God are those who live a life of justice, kindness, love and humility.[6] Thus, the opportunity to be the people of God is open to all people.

This was the core idea of the prophetic message of Amos, Micah, Jonah and all the other writers in the prophetic tradition.

Jesus was solidly set in this tradition and can be understood from no other perspective. He was ethnically a Jew. But, when the purposes of his message are understood, he becomes a human being identified with the practical life of justice, love, and humble relationships with all mankind. From this perspective, Jesus represents an utter rejection of sacrifice as a device to please God or deal with the problem of sin.

To Jews in the prophetic tradition, positive, loving, redemptive relationships were the dynamics that create whole human beings. These were the kinds of relationships that lay at the core of divine intentions for the human race.

This was surely a message the Messiah would bring to the human race. Jesus was clearly in this school of thought.

The Jewish prophetic thinkers were not the only people in the world concerned with such ethical matters. They had much in common with a multitude of social thinkers who had struggled for centuries with the dilemmas of humanity. Humans were individuals with selfish propensities and individual needs. Humans were part of God's creation needing redemptive creative social interaction to become whole human beings. Through many millennia, ideas and thoughts had been generated to solve the problems produced by the contradictions and tensions of this individual-societal interdependence.

A vast wisdom literature had developed reporting the conclusions of this intellectual work relative to the nature of spiritual and moral behavior of humans in social context. This literature appeared in written and oral form and, with additions from Jewish thinkers, was part of Jewish culture.

This was Jesus' world and this mix of culture and beliefs forged his personal identity and generated his purpose in life. His companions in his early intellectual work were people of this culture. Jesus' teachings were obviously of an ethical and moral nature. His stories and moral dictums speak directly to personal and communal behavior patterns.

Many New Testament scholars point to these moral dictums as the only remnants of the thought and teaching of Jesus. These teachings have implications for positive, redemptive social relations for all mankind and the entire world. They are messianic in the sense that they continue the conviction of the prophetic materials related to the moral and ethical stance of the creative social universe.

We find these ethical themes even more clearly enunciated in some non-canonical gospels, where the earliest reports of Jesus' work and teaching are lodged[7]. In the best of these materials there is essentially nothing of the political messianic and sacrificial ideas, which are so prominent in the canonical gospels and so central to medieval and contemporary fundamentalist theology.

To apply the priestly understanding of the messianic myth to Jesus is the antithesis of everything he lived and taught. He had clearly rejected both the nationalistic and sacrificial dimensions of that tradition. He identified with the prophetic tradition and its message of universal love and justice.

The application of the sacrificial messianic myth to Jesus is the product of literary work done two generations after Jesus' death. The problem was compounded by the theological work of the ante Nicene fathers, which culminated in the Nicene counsel in 325 CE. This church conclave, when selecting the materials to be included in the New Testament, made an arbitrary selection of these very late materials that emphasized the priestly interpretation of the messianic myth. In so doing, they excluded other writings that tended to emphasize the prophetic tradition.

It is the literal interpretation of these scriptures, which were emphasized in the second, third and fourth centuries, that distorted the life and work of Jesus. It was these distortions that made Jesus irrelevant to the medieval church and to much of modern Christianity.

These priestly political and sacrificial conceptions of the Messiah were carried over to the Christ of Christianity. To identify Jesus with this political "Christ" is a perversion with diabolical consequences. To link the real human Jesus, the dynamic teacher of human ethical responsibility, with the mythical political sacrificial "Christ" is fraught with pitfalls. Contemporary Christianity is deeply caught in this quagmire.

## CHAPTER 3

# GREEK ELEMENTS IN CHRISTIANITY

By the time of Jesus the classical period of Greek philosophy had long passed. The logical and rational disciplines promoted by Plato and Socrates was present in intellectual circles, but had little influence on the masses. Popular culture in Jesus' time was more reminiscent of the mythical world of Homer with its plethora of gods, human-divine beings, heroes, men of renown and heroic deeds. These and similar myths were a pervasive influence in all of the Near East in the early centuries CE.

Among the many categories of myths in this period, six were of particular importance in the formation of Christianity. These are: myths of divine/human cohabitation; myths of divine-human beings; myths of physical resurrection; multiple myths related to sacrifices; myths related to purification and myths indicating transitions to the supernatural world. The essential elements of these myths impacted early Christianity and were increasingly imbedded in the theological formulations of the ante Nicene church.

In the Greco-Aramaic culture there was no clear distinction made between heroic human beings and the deities. It was possible to pass between these two realms in either direction. The heroes of Mount Olympus were at once both human and divine, depending on circumstances.

The virgin birth story is foundational to some forms of Christianity. It is the rationale for the creedal doctrine of the divinity of Christ. Two Gospels of the New Testament report that Mary was pregnant as a consequence of a union with a divine being. The cohabitation of gods with human women was a common idea for millennia in Eastern religious systems. The offspring of these unions were recognized as "great men," "giants" or "heroes." One example of this myth is found in an early Hebrew tradition. In the book of Genesis a summary of the myth appears in the quotation: "The sons of God saw that the daughters of men were fair, they took to wife such of them as they chose."[8] Even more explicit is the observation: "When the sons of God came into the daughters of men and they bore children to them. These were the mighty men that were of old, the men of renown."[9]

Luke's account of the impregnation of Mary reflects this common, ancient, Near Eastern theme: "The Holy Spirit will come upon you and the power of the most High will overshadow you."[10] To think this language is not talking about a sexual union is naive beyond question. It is an exact parallel of the Genesis myth. Also parallel is the observation: "The child to be born will be called holy, the son of God."[11]

The notion of a God-man certainly was not strange to first-century people. The average person surely would admit he was only human. But the designation was not so clear in the case of powerful leaders such as kings and governors who controlled the daily fortunes of the populace. The leaders were human but, from the viewpoint of the common people, they were remarkable humans. They could be more than human. A distinction between powerful leaders, men of renown, heroes and divine beings was essentially nonexistent.[12]

Were these beings powerful because they were divine or were they divine because they were powerful? The answer to these questions was never clear.

Jesus went about teaching and preaching and gathered a following. He was obviously a great man. By the second generation his followers viewed him as a remarkable leader, the founder of a remarkable movement, a man of renown, a hero.

In the intellectual context of their world, deification of Jesus was an easy, logical progression. It was a natural attribution. Jesus was a son of God. Jesus was a God. These conclusions were inevitable in the social world of the time.

We must understand the first-century world for what it was. To import first-century literal mystical formulations into 21st-century thought is irrational. For the New Testament to have relevance for our lives today, we must first see it in the context of the world in which it was written. We must strip away the controlling religious myths. Only then will the real work and life of Jesus have dynamic relevance to us. Only then can the New Testament and Jesus be taken seriously. Only then can they be understood and made relevant to our world.

After 20 centuries we can, and we do, describe the life and teachings of Jesus as the work of a giant, a man of renown. His influence reaches over centuries and his message of love, ethical relationships, forgiveness and compassion is a dynamic moral and ethical insight. He was a man before his day, or more exactly, a man for all days. He surely summarized the core dynamics of human transformation. His teachings are confirmed by the best insights of modern social sciences.

The power of this spirit of love is the only way in which a human organism can grow into a full, complete human being. It is the only practical way in which enemies can be changed to friends; it is the only way crippled lives and emotions can be healed. Jesus, in his positive proactive spirit of love, exposes the utter folly of injustice and violence.

Surely such teaching and such a life are the work of a divine giant. In historical perspective, Jesus' life of practical love preceded his divinity, not the other way around.

Resurrection myths were also critical in the formation of Christianity. The reconstitution of the Egyptian God Osirus, after the frantic search by his wife Isis, is one of the many myths reflecting the power of the gods to rise through and above the mortality of the merely human. Gods were immortal and they had the power to resurrect humans and make them immortal.[13] Stories of the physical resurrection of Jesus are largely absent from the non-canonical gospels. They do appear, almost as an afterthought, in the canonical gospels. The selection of the four gospels we have in the New Testament was done by the church bishops at the Council of Nicaea in 325 CE. Some scholars have suggested these writings were selected because they supported the mystical Christ ideas that had become the standard dogma of the fourth-century church.

Although the question of the resurrection seemed to be settled in the creeds of the fourth and fifth centuries, it remained a subject of debate even into 21st-century churches. There have always been non-literal ways of understanding the resurrection myth and its application to Jesus.

Given the awe, reverence and admiration inspired by the life and martyr death of Jesus, it takes little imagination to understand the disciples interest in reconstituting their community and achieving unity in the same spirit they had experienced earlier. This resurrection of community was a dynamic spiritual reality for them. We, likewise, affirm this kind of resurrection when we declare that Jesus is alive in his followers today.

But these observations about the mythical ideas of divinity, virgin birth or resurrection fail to probe the most critical element in the transition from the Christianity of Jesus to the Christianity of contemporary Christian religious fundamentalism. This element is the problem of sin and its consequences. The world is full of myths relative to this matter. Why were these myths necessary in the ancient world and why do they seem so necessary in our world today?

The human being is hounded by many problems. In the first place we are caught in the agonizing mystery and uncontrollable nature of the unknowable universe. In the second place we are faced with disorder in the real social and physical worlds in which we live. To be at odds with either the supernatural or the natural order of things is painful, traumatic and destructive. The disorder in either of these realms may be described by the religious term "sin". How do individuals and societies deal with the problem of sin?

Sacrificial systems are almost universal in the cultures of the world. Sacrifices, it is believed, have effects in the supernatural world and also in the natural world. Deities and spirits interact with other powers in the supernatural world, but they also interact with this world and work through their representatives. To have good order in this world it is crucial for humans to remain on good terms with the supernatural world and its representatives. Sacrifices are designed to attain this end.

How do sacrifices establish or restore good relations with the supernatural world?

Deities tend to have characteristics like humans. This is obvious, given their origins.[14] We need only observe the behavior of the lords of this earth to understand the behavior of the lords of the supernatural world. If they don't get what they want they become hostile and prone to conflict. Conflict, disorder and disruptive behavior in one realm has co-related consequences in the other.

The only way to restore order is to satisfy the deities. They must be served and thus placated, so that they will again be well disposed to their fellow gods and to the human world.

What do the gods want? Of course, they want what humans want. They want their needs met and they want a future. Thus, at the core of sacrifice is the surrender of needed things, valued things. Things which are necessary for life and its continuance.

The kinds of sacrifice can range from food stuffs and animals to that which is critical to the survival of society: young men and pubescent women. The gods want these things and if satisfied will ensure the continuation of human society. Thus, sacrifice is an insurance premium to guarantee freedom from societal dissolution.

Sacrifice of food stuffs is universal in agricultural societies. But the sacrifice of animals had an additional significance far exceeding the mere offering of valued things. All peoples know that blood and life are inextricably connected. The sacrifice of an animal was, in this sense, the giving of life to the service of the deity. It was a symbol of a human's commitment to serve the supernatural world.

But there is another dimension to the practice of blood sacrifice and one which ultimately supercedes the idea of service.

The primary concern of all human beings is to live in a condition of well-being, a condition in which an ordered and predictable life is possible. The realization of this hope is always problematic. Disorder can arise from two sources. Humans may offend the gods and thus produce disorder in the supernatural world. The gods then project disorder back to the world of the humans who caused the problems. On the other hand, humans may engage in disruptive behavior in their communities and cause disorder in social relations. In either case "sin" has occurred. The community experiences stress and the individual committing the sin experiences guilt. Both the community and the individual are thus threatened with disintegration.

What can be done about these problems of disorder, this problem of sin? What can be done about the inevitable stress and possible societal and individual dissolution?

Action must be taken to restore order. Both the community and the sinner must take some action in order to undo the sin. The solution has two foci: the sinner must be punished and the sinner must be restored to the community.

The sinner has damaged the community and is no longer worthy to be a member. He must be removed. Ideally this should be a real death, which is accomplished in some instances by capital punishment. However, this has traumatic consequences for families and the whole community.

The sacrificial system provides an alternative way of removing the offender, and religion is the institution in which the alternative is applied. The offending individual is killed, but only forensically. A substitute is appointed and killed. Thus, the offender is symbolically removed from the community, and the community is cleansed and freed from the offender. As far as the supernatural world is concerned, the sinner has been adequately punished. The anger of the gods is assuaged and order restored.

In this forensic drama the sinner is symbolically gone. But, in reality, the person is still there.

What is that person to do? What is his community to do? He has offended the community, become alienated from it, and is isolated in the terrible anxiety of his own guilt. It would be much better to be dead; but he isn't.

What can be done to free the person from guilt? What can be done to restore the person to the community?

The blood of the sacrifice has a symbolic cleansing effect. The real person who was defiled by his sin is symbolically purified. He is no longer responsible for the sin and thus is freed from guilt. The person, now sinless, can be restored to the community. The blood component of sacrifice thus has two interrelated effects. The individual is saved from the consequences of sin and is at the same time restored to the community. A purification and a rebirth have occurred.

There is in effect a symbolic resurrection, but more importantly a de facto social resurrection.

All of this may sound familiar to those who are acquainted with American religious fundamentalism. But it was all familiar to the mystery religions of the Near East long before Jesus or the New Testament.

An example of this genre of sacrifice common in Asia Minor at the time of the formation of Christianity was the Taurobolium. In this ritual, a bull was slaughtered on a latticework of poles constructed over a pit. Those who wanted reconciliation with the supernatural world and their fellow men stood or knelt in the bottom of the pit. The bull was killed, and the penitents lifted their faces upward, allowing the blood to run into their mouths and flow down over their bodies.[15] As the blood washed over their bodies they were symbolically cleansed from all their offences. A new life was initiated. Thus, they were restored to favor with the supernatural world and the community.

The power of this ritual in placating and cementing relations with the supernatural world, and its cleansing, purifying and restorative efficacy with the local community, was not lost on the second and third generation followers of Jesus.

By the early part of the second century the heroic dimensions of Jesus were well developed and his divinity established. The death of Jesus, in retrospect, took on the role of a sacrifice – a blood sacrifice. But a sacrifice far more significant than any sacrifice in Jewish tradition or the blood sacrifices of the mystery religions of the Greco-Roman world. This interpretation of the death of Jesus provided a dynamic rationale for his death. The crucifixion of the God-man was an adequate punishment for the sin of all mankind. The blood of the God-man spilled at the crucifixion washed away the sin and expunged the guilt of all mankind. The crucifixion in this sacrificial sense took a central crucial role in the new religion.

The power of the crucifixion grew as Christianity became obsessed with the problem of sin and its absolution. As the church emphasized sin and its consequent terrors in the future world, the crucifixion became a dynamic instrument for social control. The theory of the substitutionary atoning sacrificial death of Jesus was essentially formulated by the time of the creeds in the fourth and fifth centuries. It was elaborated in the medieval church and generally fixed by Anselm in the 11th century.

The life and teachings of Jesus have nothing in common with this creedal doctrine or Anselm's formulation. However, a profoundly confusing connection and perversion has been made.

Jesus lived and taught an ethical way of life. He was concerned with the quality of interpersonal relations and he asked his followers to follow in this way. It was a demanding ethical standard.

How could one live up to such a standard. One could succeed in some measure but failure was almost certain for the average human being. Failing followers felt the pain of their failing. They had betrayed their leader.

So how does one deal with this "failing"? The sacrificial mystery religions had been dealing with this problem since the beginning of time.

It was an easy step for the followers of Jesus to convert the death of their leader into the supreme sacrifice of all time. Surely the blood of the God-man was ultimately powerful in purging sin and removing guilt.

It is an inviting idea. The sinner could be saved. Is it any wonder that the substitutionary atonement type of Christianity became popular in the early centuries of our era and even appeals to many people to this day?

But none of this theory has anything to do with the real Jesus. It has everything to do with the mystery religions which influenced and ultimately formed the Christianity of the fourth century, medieval Christianity and modern Christian fundamentalism.

## CHAPTER 4

# CHRISTIANITY AND THE ROMAN CONTEXT

The Christian church, by the second century, was expanding beyond Asia Minor into Europe – the more Roman segment of the world. Converts were increasingly citizens or inhabitants of the Empire. They were socialized in Roman ways with Roman values and Roman understandings of both this world and the supernatural world. They could no more escape their culture than we can escape ours.

Pax Romana provided the communication and tranquility for ideas to travel and cultural change to occur. In this context Christianity flourished, but as it flourished it was changed by the dynamic characteristics of its new environment. Two critical features of Roman culture modified Christianity. One was the religious system, particularly the traditional beliefs and practices among the masses of the peasant population. The second was the pattern of social organization.

The official Roman religion had been influenced by Greek religious ideas. Consequently their gods shared similar characteristics and functions but differed in names. For example, Jupiter in Roman theology was similar to Zeus in the Greek pantheon.

But a more spiritual religion existed among the masses. In contrast to the Greek and official Roman anthropomorphic deities, the supernatural beings trusted by rural Romans tended to be spirits. These spirits were local and directly related to the events and needs of everyday life. They manifested themselves in real, practical effects for the common people.

The peasants depended on these spirits for all the various needs of life. Security of the community, stable social life, the health of individuals, and the well being of crops and animals all depended on the beneficent actions of the spirits. But the spirits did not supply the gift of the good life unilaterally or freely.

The good life depended on the right relationship between humans and spirits. These relationships were essentially bargaining arrangements. Although the spirits were supernatural and more powerful than humans, their power was limited and problematic. And these limitations were inextricably bound up with the people individually and corporately. The people depended on the goodwill and power of the spirits but the spirits, in turn, depended on the services of the humans in order to maintain their power.

This power was assured, restored and increased only if the peasants provided gifts and various other services. These gifts and services contributed to the power of the spirits, and thus enabled them to provide things necessary for physical and social sustenance in the human community.

The contractual arrangement is clearly stated in a typical incantation recited as a central feature of the religious sacrificial ceremonies. This incantation "Do ut des" means essentially "I give so that you may give."[16]

Failure to provide services to the spirits decreased their ability to provide welfare for the community. Obviously people and spirits were bound together in a strong reciprocal relationship. This "boundedness" is crucial in the forms of Roman religion which impacted the development of Christianity. The verb "to bind" is "religare" and is the root of the word "religion." Thus, religion is a contract relationship with the spirit world. The people, if they wished to live and prosper, were bound to provide services to the spirits.[17]

The spirits, although supernatural, were local, not far off in some distant heaven. The services they required were immediate, direct and personal. This form of Roman religion was neither creedal nor moral; it was contractual. The spirits could and would supply necessary elements of the good life, but only if humans provided the required services.

These services were of two principle kinds. One kind consisted of offering things valued in an agricultural community. The spirits, it was assumed, needed the things that humans need: grains, fruits, vegetables, bread, etc. Animals also might be offered, but blood sacrifice did not have the same propitiatory significance as in the Greek mystery religions.

The second kind of service was a set of more ritualistic ceremonies and incantations very much akin to the principles of magic. To be effective with the spirits these rituals had to be performed correctly. Thus, they could be done only by well-trained practitioners schooled in the intricacies of the rites and well practiced in the proper intonations of the incantations. An atmosphere of reverence, piety and fear were the only conceivable human responses in the context of these realities. Life was a serious matter when one was daily in the presence of spirits whose goodwill determined the conditions of both physical and social life.

There was always the danger that a stranger might gain knowledge of the rituals and perform them inappropriately, thus incurring wrath rather than blessing from the spirits. The rituals were even more secure if they had secret dimensions entrusted only to appropriate practitioners. The moral and ethical character of the officiating priest and common participants was irrelevant. The careful performance of rituals and meticulous recitation of the formulas were the essence of service to the spirits.

The Roman converts to Christianity had been taught a Christianity created by the mix of ideas inspired by the priestly tradition of the Jewish Diaspora and multiple elements from Greek mystery religions. To this mix of Christianity, Roman culture contributed these contractual conceptions of reciprocal relations with the world of the spirits.

The forms of service to the spirit world changed through the centuries, but the concept inspired the creation of rituals and incantations in the medieval church. In our day, the Sunday morning service, the evening service, the Wednesday evening service, holy day services, song service and all other forms of service reflect this traditional Roman understanding and practice of service to the spirits of the supernatural world.

A worshipful atmosphere expresses reverence – a pious demeanor in the presence of the spirits is essential. The practices of reading sacred literature, singing hymns, giving offerings, preaching a sermon, officiating at mass, participating in liturgical reading, reciting the creeds are all understood as service activities. Some Christians still believe such services will please the supernatural world and result in blessings to the individual and community. Some Christians think the highest form of service is the creation of new worship communities which then provide more services to the supernatural world.

Jesus' emphasis on dynamic love and ethical behavior

almost disappeared as Christianity moved into Europe and amalgamated with Roman religious culture.

The second major Roman influence which brought dramatic change to the theology and life of the developing church was the hierarchical nature of the political and military institutions of that society.

The application of Roman law and military power produced a stable society and several centuries of social order. This system was relatively free from the capricious and arbitrary acts of unstable dictators. The Roman emperor was powerful, but ideally he was not beyond the constraints of the senate. The Empire was, for administrative purposes, divided into provinces.

All aspects of society were arranged in an hierarchical way. Official administrative duties and powers were allocated vertically. In this bureaucracy, directives flowed downward and information and questions moved upward. A rigid adherence to law was deeply engrained in the culture. Every level of society had its obligations. Roles were clearly defined. Both custom and law required conformity.

Emperor, senators, citizens, serfs and slaves knew the system, knew their place in it and engaged the power structures at the appropriate level. Rigid attention to the law created a disciplined population. Any individualistic challenge to the order of things was fraught with great danger.

Undergirding the system was a vast but disciplined military institution. Conformity to social norms was expected, but coercion was an ever-present last resort. The lower one was on the hierarchical scale, the greater was the importance of fear as an instrument of order. Coercion and punishment were never far away. Official violence was designed to terrify people into obedience.

These features of the Roman Empire: hierarchical order of authority, bureaucratic structure, legal requirements and coercion became the model for the organization of the church as it matured in the western world. The converts to Christianity grew up in this ordered system. The church leaders appreciated its administrative efficiency, order, stability and efficacy in social control and church discipline.

As the church developed, the geographical regions of its influence were divided into religious provinces. Church diplomats carried diplomatic pouches with secret documents between the church headquarters in Rome and the various archdiocese.

The Pope was the religious version of the Roman Emperor. The conclave of cardinals was the religious version of the Roman senate.

The power of the spiritual hierarchy extended from God at the apex, through Christ at his right hand, to Christ's vicar on earth, and then downward through archbishops, bishops, priests and lesser officials. Persons in the earthly segment of this hierarchy were the powerful people in the church. In some senses, they were the church and came to be known as the "religious."

The "religious" had two different roles. One was to administer the worldly structures of the church, including construction and care of cathedrals, church building and staffing. The second role was a contractual interdependent relationship with and service to the supernatural world. The "religious" provided services to the supernatural world, and were also conduits of the blessings of that world and its powers to the people.

In their conversion to Christianity, the Roman converts had inherited the blood sacrificial doctrines, which had formed the core of Christianity in Asia Minor. They were immersed in the mysteries of the cross, the miraculous saving blood sacrifice of the God-man, and the imponderables of resurrection and ascension.

These crucial ideas and practices were incorporated and formalized into a vast and complex system of services in the Roman church. The officials of the hierarchy offered the sacrifices, performed the rituals and controlled the secrets of the church. They acted as intermediaries between the people and the supernatural world. They communicated the truths of the supernatural world and dispensed grace to communicants. They instructed people in the proper service to God and the saints and demonstrated appropriate reverence and piety in the presence of the supernatural world.

Participation of the communicants was limited to two dimensions. In the physical dimension they were expected to serve the hierarchy in numerous ways. In the spiritual dimension they were expected to observe the ceremony of the mass, make confessions, take communion and participate in the liturgy.

Thus, the common people were separated from the deities by a whole coterie of religious functionaries who held the secrets of the supernatural and dispensed its favors as they chose. This kind of organization and hierarchical structure was a direct copy of the Roman social system. Obedience and conformity to the religious institution was inspired by fear - again a direct reflection of Roman social order.

How did the church fit Jesus into this theological and social system?

Since the hierarchy was a power structure, Jesus, as founder of the church, was primary. Had he not died for its establishment? Was he not its ultimate man of renown? After all, he was a God-man. By the second century, Jesus the Christ dwelt in the supernatural world and was at the right hand of God. The actual administration of the church was on earth, and the power and gifts flowed from heaven to the church on earth through a representative – Christ's vicar the pope – and then down through the lower levels of the hierarchy.

The supernatural world was the abode and domain of Christ and of God. But it also had a vast array of unknown demons, malevolent spirits, fearsome, fickle and angry spiritual beings. In the final analysis, God – the final judge – was to be feared more than all the other spiritual entities of that unknown world.

The certainty and terror of supernatural judgment and eternal suffering were ever-present realities for the masses. What could the average person do?

There was only one way to escape the spiritual terrors and that way was controlled by the intermediaries who had contact with Jesus the Christ and God. An appeal to the powers of this spiritual legal system at the accessible, appropriate level was the only way of escape.

This method of handling spiritual terror is not unique to the medieval church. The protestant reformation left the top intact. In the protestant system, the human in awe and fear of the supernatural power must appeal to Christ, for there is no other power or deity to save one from the ultimate terrors of the unknowable supernatural world.

Can a greater perversion of Jesus' purpose, life and message be imagined? Yet some segments of contemporary Christianity manage this perversion and promote it with absolute certainty.

## CHAPTER 5

# THE GOOD NEWS CONTINUES

Now we must return to the fourth decade of the first century.

Jesus was crucified! Jesus was dead and buried. His followers were devastated!

They had given up much from their ethnic cultural past. At first they surrendered tentatively and then more assuredly as they came to sense the creative dynamic of Jesus' teaching of a universal ethic. They sensed, in the message of Jesus, a contact with fundamental social laws of the universe.

They had experienced him as a great teacher. But he was much more than a teacher. He was a model of real personal and social redemption. A creative human being able to excite people of all kinds to embark on lives of serious ethical commitment.

He had given them the courage to leave the rituals of the past and discard the oppressive demands of religious form. He had provided the vision of a way to a fuller humanity through positive interactive processes of love and forgiveness. He had demonstrated what it meant to be truly and fully human. They had cautiously and haltingly embarked on this path with him. In this new ethical order they glimpsed a view of the social world in which all categories of people could become equally human and capable of realizing the potential of their humanity. This was indeed the way to freedom. This way was the way to salvation.

This was Jesus' work and vision. This was his followers' hope. They were immature in their understanding, but they were on their way.

But Jesus was dead!

What were they to do without a guide? What would happen to their vision? What would happen to the teachings? What did these teachings and stories really mean in the stark cold world? Those who had heard the teachings as they walked with Jesus on the pathways of the countryside and the villages of Galilee were in a quandary. And what about the hopes of those who had not known Jesus, but had heard of the stories and teachings from friends and passersby?

Jesus was dead!

Those who had feared the teachings of Jesus may have been relieved. The Jewish traditionalists had eliminated a challenge. The Romans had eliminated a troublemaker who talked about love rather than violence as a way to structure society, provide order and guide human relationships.

But, for those who had given their lives to Jesus, there was disillusionment. What should they do now? What of the message? What of the hope? What of the social movement which, they thought, had the potential to redeem and renovate the world?

The swirl of ideas and convictions was far from disappearing. Jesus was gone but the followers were alive. They gathered, debated and discussed the meaning of their experiences. They recalled the stories, parables and wise sayings of Jesus. But they also recalled their Jewish history and heritage, which had formed essential aspects of their identity and sense of selfhood.

For them, as for all Jews, conceptions of Monotheism and Messiah were at the core of their life. The meaning of the Messiah was uncertain. In the priestly tradition, there was an expectation of a supernatural intervention to reestablish a Jewish state. In the prophetic tradition, the Messiah was perceived as a messenger of ethical concerns. These two extremes, with many types of shading, were also the subject of debate and speculation among Jesus' followers. By the end of the first century the four gospels and the writings of Paul still reflected both priestly and prophetic traditions.

Some followers of Jesus had a bias toward the priestly tradition, which became more pronounced as the early church fathers emphasized the supernatural dimensions of the stories about Jesus. These ideas led, ultimately, to the construction of the "Christ" of the creeds. Other disciples and followers, more attune to the prophetic tradition, repudiated all notions of a special people, in a special land, with a special political destiny and they rejected all sacrificial notions of religion. For them God's people were those who had a special quality of life – a life in which love, justice and peace were central. From this perspective all people could be God's people.

What was the meaning of it all? In the context of such a culture, what was the meaning of Jesus' life and teachings?

Some simply went back to their old ways.

For the committed and the curious, such a course was impossible. Among the most insightful, there was a growing awareness of a critical fact: Jesus' message had a dynamic of its own. It was no longer dependent on the physical presence of the master teacher and storyteller. It no longer depended on the remarkable demonstration of Jesus' daily behavior marked by compassion as he walked among friends and enemies. His ethical way of life, the consummate incarnation of love, could go on without its teacher. Jesus had begun a social movement, which incarnated an ethic capable of revolutionizing social and personal life even without him.

It was a social movement independent of any cultural heritage for it was a way of life for all humanity. It was a call to all human beings to forsake their tribal and ethnic exclusiveness. It was a call to a radical ethic of personal and social renovation. It was a way to rise to a fuller humanity than had ever been experienced in the social evolution of the human race. Jesus had shown the way to life – true, full, human life. This was salvation from the devastating, dehumanizing impact of separateness and fear. It was the way to heal the dislocations and alienations in the personal and social life of any community, tribe or nation. It was a call to join the human race and experience its potential.

Those who had penetrated most deeply into the message of Jesus understood this call to an ethical social revolution. Thus, the movement could go on for it was larger than any leader. This spiritual movement needed no physical resurrection for it was resurrected in every person who dared to forsake past securities and join in redemptive social interaction.

In this sense the essential work and life of Jesus had not died. It could go on living and growing in all those who committed themselves to his way. The lives of the followers would be a continuing revelation of the essential core of the ethical structure of the universe. Jesus had incarnated this moral and ethical spirit. His followers could do the same.

Freedom from the constraints of pharisaic legalisms and narrow ethnic self-righteousness was an exhilarating experience. Dynamic love in a community of mutual responsibility was surely a new approach to the problems of human existence. The marvel and excitement of freedom from the confusing and terrifying mysteries of the supernatural world made possible a confidence in the capacity of love to change the world.

The central task of the followers was to make clear the continuity of Jesus' message and life in their own lives. They found themselves called not only to live the life of Jesus, but also to report that life so others might participate in social creation and human renovation. The ethical order of social relations in the universe was now clear in a completeness never known before. Jesus had shown the way in his life and teachings. Jesus' followers had found freedom in a new understanding of God's nature and work.

They discovered their real mission and purpose of life in the sharing of this good news. Jesus, in his essence, lived on. He lived on in those who incarnated his life in generation after generation.

For these followers of Jesus, the mystical, fantastic supernatural world and its magical intrusions were irrelevant – indeed, a barrier to the wholeness of life. They were saved from the fearsome anxiety associated with deities, demons and mysterious forces which tradition had taught them. They were saved from the burdensome, but utterly ineffectual, magic of rituals and sacrifices, which the traditional supernatural world had demanded in traditional religion.

This was good news. This is good news. This is the gospel.

## CHAPTER 6

# THE EVOLUTION OF THE "MAN" JESUS INTO THE "MYTHICAL CHRIST"

Certainly there was enough in the life of Jesus to set him apart from the average man.

But how did the spare, stark, down-to-earth teacher and practitioner of an ethic of love turn into the creedal Christ of the fourth century? How did the dynamic story-telling preacher of the Galilean countryside turn into the ritualistic, sacrificial savior of medieval and modern Christianity?

How did the essential facts of Jesus' life and his ethical teachings come to be obscured and pushed into the background? Why did mystical and miraculous elements come to be attributed to him? How did three years of ministry and the work of his life disappear and a few incomprehensible supernatural intrusions take center stage? How did the humble carpenter of the first century come to be encrusted by fantastic embellishments, which appear in the canonical gospels two generations after his death?

How did all these come to be incorporated into the central dogmas of a vast religious system? How did his name come to be associated with a system of thought and a ponderous social structure, which is antithetical to everything he taught and lived? How did the "man" Jesus turn into the "mythical Christ" of 21st-century Christian orthodoxy?

These questions demand answers if we hope to understand the Jesus who underlies true redemptive Christianity.

Apparently not all the followers of Jesus were able to penetrate the depth of his purpose and work. The ethical demands were startling, maybe unattainable in the normal flow of things. Some could not escape the pull of tradition and the comfort of the usual. Jesus had called them to forsake all that was familiar in the supernatural world and its cultural representations. Such a conversion took tremendous courage. It was painful to discard what had been so meaningful in the face of a world filled with mystery, pain and uncertainty.

Maybe it was too much to ask them to reject the political hopes of their heritage or the fantastic, magical, sacrificial dimensions of Greek culture surrounding them. Maybe it was inevitable that a merging of Jesus with mythical images and beliefs would occur as time passed and memories of his ethical teachings faded.

We must have some sympathy for their dilemma.

Maybe there was, they thought, some way in which their experiences with Jesus and knowledge of his teachings could be merged with the symbols, images and beliefs, which had formed them in their Jewish-Aramaic culture?

Jesus was a public figure. Stories about him and his teachings continued to circulate after this death. People wanted to know more about him. His ministry, popularity and death all needed explanation.

Stories developed, interpretations were made. For at least a generation the information was largely oral. Wherever there were ready listeners, the stories were told and retold. Jewish communities in Palestine and the Diaspora were the first to hear. Then Gentiles. Since the search for truth and hope is timeless and universal, the marvelous stories gained a hearing.

As these were retold through innumerable minds and mouths, how did the content and form of the stories change? What variations, exclusions, embellishments and additions occurred? What sharpening and elaborations took place as the stories were enfolded in the cultures of the Near East? In what way did the experiences and beliefs of common people produce modifications? In what way did the regional ideas of diverse communities and cultures color the retelling? What local myths provided the means of interpretation and the creation of meaning?

This was not a scientific world. Neither was it a world where the strict cannons of modern historiography were practiced. The Near Eastern cultures were dominated by ideas of supernatural intrusions, miraculous happenings and sacrificial placation. Surely the most prosaic aspects of Jesus' biography could not escape reformulations consistent with the central motifs of the Jewish, Greek and Roman cultures in which they were told.

As the stories were being rehearsed and reconstructed, people were grappling with the meaning and significance of Jesus' life, ministry and death. For some, a sense of his greatness and uniqueness began to dawn. Here indeed was a notable man, a man of renown, a giant of a man. As the stories reached a population that had not known Jesus in his lifetime, his reputation needed explanation.

The earliest known attempts to do this are the letters of Paul. Paul had not known Jesus personally. For whatever reason – psychological or theological – he had been converted from an enemy of the Jesus cult to a follower.

Paul, like some of the early followers of Jesus, might have sensed a continuity of Jesus' spirit living on in their communities. Surely this spirit lived on in the dynamic moral and ethical formulations, which brought creative and redemptive life to humans.

Did Paul understand that Jesus had successfully connected the ethics of love with the wisdom literature of the ages and with the prophetic understanding of the Messiah? If he did, then he understood that Jesus – the messenger, the Christ – was living and present in the communities established by the preaching of the good news. In this sense, Jesus had been resurrected.

Paul's letters may reflect this conviction in phrases such as "God is in you," "you are in God," "Christ is in you," and "you are in Christ." If this view is correct, God – for Paul – was right there, alive and living in the loving redemptive life of real human beings. Christ was really alive in the community.

Based on this interpretation, there is nothing mystical or supernatural in the phrases quoted above. Paul is simply declaring a conviction that a creative, redemptive, principle of human interaction really works in the community of people who follow in the way of Jesus. It was a principle of human interaction far greater and more dynamic than the interactions promoted by traditional mystery religions, cold pharisaical rituals and routines, or fantastic spiritual suppositions.

If this is indeed Paul's meaning, it is a profound insight that Christians should rediscover in this 21st century.

But Paul had a very complicated understanding of Jesus. Paul was not only a Greco-Jew, but also a Roman of Asia Minor. This writer of letters, it is abundantly evident, understood Jesus in a way marvelously consistent with his culture. We must remember that Paul was a native of the city of Tarsus, a hotbed of intellectual ferment as well as a region of stolid traditional religious and spiritual tradition. He was a product of first-century Asia Minor, intimately acquainted with the common myths of the time and formally educated in Greek and Roman thought patterns.

The amalgam of all this formed Paul's life and worldview. How did he put Jesus together with this cultural understanding of the world. In Paul's letter we find words and phrases that express fundamental philosophies, religious dogmas and theologies as old as Persian Mithranism and its Zoroastrian version.

This philosophical system was well established in Tarsus by 390 BCE and dominant in Asia Minor and the near East by the first century CE. There is no way in which Saul of Tarsus could have escaped the impact of this complex system of thought, with its extensive sacrificial system, purification rituals and disciplined, moral, behavioral system.[18]

It was a ready-made framework for any person living in the Near Eastern culture to understand and interpret the more mystical and miraculous elements of the stories about Jesus, which had emerged by the seventh decade of the first century. Paul's interpretation of the life, and particularly the death of Jesus, reflects the core ideas of the religion that surrounded him in the days of his youth.

People of Asia Minor, in their heritage, were intimately acquainted and emotionally involved with traditional ideas[19] such as: virgin births, God-men, purification rites by blood sacrifices, ideas of resurrection and belief in a union with the supernatural after death. For Jews in the Diaspora, the coming of the Messiah was important. But similar expectations were present in ancient Persian mythology and were present in Near Eastern thought many centuries before the Common Era.

Many terms used in Christianity reflect an intimacy with ancient eastern thought: resurrection, new birth, purification, holy place, priest of good things to come, blood sacrifice, sanctification and eternal spirit.

All this characterized the worldview, the frame of reference, the screen of meaning for many people in the region. This was the very population to whom Paul felt a special mission and with whom he was the most successful.

Paul lived in a real world. If we are to understand his writing we must see his interpretations of Jesus in the cultural context in which he was formed and the cultural context of the churches he founded in the Roman empire.

If we take this perspective, a problem with the Pauline materials emerge. Are there two contradictory theologies present in Paul? It would seem so! Some have designated these two theologies as Judaic Christianity and Hellenistic Christianity.

The quintessential statement in the book of Hebrews,[20] if taken seriously, reflects the core of Mithraic doctrine in its Greek version. The framework of an ancient literal theology is there and Jesus is pressed into this philosophical and religious mold. Both Paul and his readers would have felt at home with this interpretation. It was already their culture.

Jesus in his death, the God-man sacrifice, fulfilled their expectations and provided an immediate and up-to-date theology.

From Paul's two-fold interpretation of Jesus' life and death emerges a theological system fraught with contradictions. Can ethical thought and crucial elements of Greek mythology be melded together? The contradictions in this attempted syncretism were evident in succeeding centuries. It provided a fertile intellectual milieu for confusion in the writers of the gospels and subsequent incendiary debates of the ante Nicene fathers.

Paul and the writer of Hebrews were not the only ones to struggle with the meaning of the life and death of Jesus. Each person who thought about these matters lived in his own real world with its cultural explanations of all aspects of life. Theologizing is inevitable. A framework for the interpretation of Jesus' life and death was at hand for each person.

There were many people who had heard Jesus preach and teach. There were many more who heard of his stories from others. These people told and retold the stories. Ultimately and inevitably they were telling their own versions of the stories and creating their own interpretations.

These oral reports of Jesus' life and work circulated widely. Their forms, of course, were not fixed and the interpretations were fluid. Certain parts of his life story were dropped, others were added, embellishments were made, sharpening occurred. Finally, by the end of the first century, elements of these materials appeared in written form. We know some of these as the canonical gospels. New Testament scholarship and archeological work in recent years have brought others to light.

The similarities in some of the canonical gospels suggest a common written source may have been used by some of the writers. This presumed document is known as Q. Thus, it seems, both oral tradition and written materials underlay or were included in the canonical gospels, which began to appear at the end of the first century – 60 to 70 years after Jesus was crucified. By the time the canonical books received their final form, many decades later, different aspects of the story and multiple interpretations were vying for acceptance.

But that was not the end of the confusion about Jesus and his meaning.

The masses of people were not living in a rational scientific world. They were simple people used to stories of miracles and magic. Their most fervent beliefs and hopes were often bonded to myths.

For most, there was no clear distinction between "this world" and the "supernatural world." The nature of Mid-Eastern culture easily accommodated explanations of almost everything according to some supernatural and sacred formulas. The fantastic and miraculous were a necessary component of this worldview. In such a worldview the "in breaking of God" could hardly be accomplished without some indicators, some traces, of magnificent supernatural power which undergirded and formed the world in which they lived.

For the common man, in the first century Mid-Eastern culture, new beginnings, a new birth, a new society could come only under the impact of supernatural power. It should be noted that the disciples were common men.

If God did anything in this world it would be done with startling majesty and demonstrations of power trailing glory from that supernatural world. Heavenly indicators – angels, mysterious kings, magi, and the riches associated with power – were telltale signs of the presence of the supernatural.[21]

Jesus' followers were convinced he was the founder of a social movement. Such a marvelous movement could hardly be ordinary. Jesus had grown large in their eyes and larger as their memory faded. A natural birth for such a leader and founder was a manifest impossibility. A natural birth of such a person was to them as absurd as a supernatural birth seems to us.

Early followers, in addition to Paul, also attempted an analysis of Jesus' life and death. They were members of a fringe group, an ethnic minority, in a backwater enclave of the Roman world. Can a more powerless condition be imagined? How were these people to find dignity and worth and the energy to promote the social movement to which they had given their lives.

They were convinced they had become part of the moral power of the universe. From such a conviction grew the sense of linkage to the supernatural.

Their movement and its founder and leader could be explained in no other way. The writers of the canonical gospel accounts were people of this kind of culture.

Although these miraculous dimensions were not crucial to the life and work of Jesus, neither were they a hindrance to the story or its telling. An accommodation of the gospel to the world in which people lived was easy. Many manuscripts reflecting such thoughts and such interpretation were produced. The earliest of these writers and their fellow followers were called Christians by the eighth decade of the first century CE.

For those followers from the Jewish tradition, these ideas were supported, probably even generated, by a singular element in their history. Their very existence demonstrated their unique place in God's world. They were, they believed, a "divinely-called people," a people separate from all other tribes and nations. They felt they had exclusive rights and access to the only real power of the universe. Their culture, and synagogue reinforced these convictions from the moment of birth.

For them, other ethnic groups in neighboring villages and towns were not chosen people and had no special purpose. The Samaritans were of this ilk. And there were many others. Then there were the Romans, who actively exploited the minorities and the poor. What was one to think of them?

But Jesus had asked them to give up this marvelous sense of identity. He had even associated with a Samaritan and a woman at that! He had crossed cultural barriers, had broken down the walls that separated human from human, he had compromised the unique status of God's people. He went even further and made oneness with all humanity a cardinal tenet of his teaching and life.

They had given up much. They had cut themselves off from the power structures of their society. But to cut themselves off from a core component of their ancestral group and self-identity was more than some of them could bear. Their charismatic leader had gone too far. Everything in their history encouraged a perception of separateness and exclusion. This fundamental conviction, coupled with a hope that their new social movement would be powerful and play a significant role in the rapidly changing world, led to a Christianity marked by exclusiveness, intolerance and ultimately even violence.

This Jewish cultural feature appeared and reappeared even as the movement, under the missionary endeavors of Paul, expanded to the Greek and Roman worlds. Exclusiveness is a prominent feature of Western Christianity to this day and is realistically and literally encapsulated in the declaration "for there is no other name, under heaven, given to men whereby we must be saved."[22] This was a remarkable perversion of Jesus' fundamental contribution to the human social world.

Our knowledge of Jesus' life and work has been enriched by recent discoveries of stories and fragments of stories in Nag Hammadi and other ancient libraries in Egypt and the Near East. These findings have raised the number of gospel accounts and fragments of accounts to as many as 28 or 30. We have only four in the New Testament.

It is impossible to determine who wrote these canonical and non-canonical materials, and when they were written. The standards of authorship and documentation which we expect in the 21st century certainly did not exist. The names attached to any of the materials are not necessarily the authors' names. It was common practice to employ names of notable people in order to promote the reading of the letters or documents and provide an aura of credibility. It was also common practice to incorporate material from various sources without acknowledgement. Plagiarism was not considered unethical by writers at the turn of the second century.

The narratives attributed to Mark, Matthew and Luke repeat both oral and written stories as they had been shaped by the culture of the Near East in the late first century.

The Gospel of John, a theological treatise of the early second century, attempted a full-blown supernatural interpretation of Jesus. The author of this significant document was obviously conversant with and deeply immersed in the fundamentals of Greek mystery religions. The God-man model was applied to Jesus in a direct and comprehensive manner. The sacrificial atonement, purification ritual was applied to Jesus' death and made him into a supernatural sacrifice. Whether the author intended all this in a literal or symbolical sense is problematic.

The effects on the creation of Christianity, however, are very clear. These two core ideas of Greek mystery religions have been applied to Jesus in a literal sense and are the dominant themes of medieval and contemporary Christian fundamentalism.

Succeeding generations in this tradition extracted, emphasized and interpreted a number of stories found in these writings. They continued the modification, embellishment and sharpening which had occurred in the oral stage and early written stages. As they did so, the life, ministry and ethical teachings of Jesus became irrelevant.

His words and work were replaced by fantastic interpretations of five events: the annunciation, the birth, the crucifixion, the resurrection and the ascension. These events grew large in the minds of church leaders and theologians. As they worked on these themes, they created a mythical Christ and essentially discarded Jesus.

The mythical Christ of Christianity thrived and spread. But so did the controversies surrounding the interpretations of that Christ. These were so widespread and so intense they threatened the stability of the Roman Empire. Constantine convened the Council of Nicaea in 325 CE and demanded that the church bishops resolve the key points of the controversies. The result was the Nicene Creed.[23]

There were other councils and other creeds reflecting variations of interpretations, but the mythical Christ was consistently present. It is evident the Christian religion of that mystical genre was created by priests and bishops of the third and fourth centuries. It is also obvious the mythical Christ of the five events was the central figure of that religion.

Some scholars refer to this religion as Constantinian Christianity.

It is the kind of Christianity believed and practiced by the medieval church. It is still the orthodox belief of many mainline churches today and probably the majority of those who call themselves Christians. Contemporary confessions of faith or doctrinal statements, with all their revisions, have done little to change the magical dimensions of this religion.

It is a kind of Christianity which essentially rejects the life, ministry and teachings of Jesus. Jesus would not be able to identify with it and would be the first to repudiate its essence. Jesus was not and would not be a Christian in the strictures of creeds and doctrines of Constantinian Christianity.

But Jesus was a messenger, a messiah, a Christ. He founded a social movement. It is a kind of Christianity, which lives on in those who love the whole world in a redemptive way. Shall we call this kind of Christianity "Jesus Christianity"?

It is clear that Jesus Christianity and Constantinian Christianity have little in common. It is equally clear that "Jesus the Messenger of Galilee" has little in common with "the Christ" of the fourth century creeds or the doctrines of Christian religious fundamentalism.

We must recover the essential meaning of Jesus' life, ministry and death if we are to understand God's continuing work in the 21st century. To fail to do so will assign the revolutionary spiritual-ethical work of Jesus to the scrap heap of history, and doom humanity to ever-increasing cycles of violence.

Fortunately, the recovery of the historical Jesus and his life and work is possible. His social movement is not dead.

## CHAPTER 7

# CHRISTIANITY AND THE REFORMATION

Medieval Christianity, formed in the milieu of the Roman Empire, endured unchallenged for a thousand years. The hierarchical structure, with the application of both its political and mystical spiritual power, provided the coercive structure for social order.

The religious life of the period was dominated by creeds and supportive rituals. Individual Christians feared the hierarchy, observed the sacraments, participated in confession and attended mass performed by members of the "religious." These elements, not ethical behavior, guaranteed forgiveness and ultimate salvation in a supernatural domain.

The supernatural world was of ultimate concern. The individual could do nothing about either this world or the next. It was all in the hands of God and his emissaries. The fear of an eternal torturing hell and the hope of heaven were the dominant dynamics, which enabled the church to control society and the masses.

For human beings caught in this system, life in this world was a preparation for the next. Suffering, injustice, misery and oppression were the expected lot here. These conditions were to be endured because the church would take care of passage to the pleasures and glories in the next world.

In this context, ethical motivation was eclipsed. Individual and social responsibility became irrelevant. How one lived with one's fellowmen was of little concern. To the extent one violated relationships, a confession to the priest would take care of all offenses and their consequences – regardless of gravity or frequency. Renovation of life and change of behavior were incidental to the system of salvation. What was critical was not a transformed life, but mental ascent to creedal statements, obedience to the hierarchy and performance of rituals.

There were, at times, arduous efforts to come to grips with the imponderables of the creeds and dogmas of the church. There were attempts to apply the powers of the intellect to a systematic understanding of the supernatural world and its persistent intrusion into this world. There were thinkers in the medieval era and not just performers of religious rites.

One of these thinkers was Anselm, Archbishop of Canterbury who lived from 1033 to 1109. The body of knowledge he worked with hardly went beyond the pronouncements of the Church fathers, particularly Augustine, and the creeds of the fourth and fifth centuries. He accepted the basic propositions, but attempted to apply Aristotelian logic in order to create a rational system, which would support the creeds and doctrines. Most of his work continued the debate about the nature of the three aspects of the Trinity. But he had another concern.

The creeds had dealt with the problem of sinful man and salvation in a rather inconclusive way. The general import of the creeds relative to this matter may be summed up in the observations: "Christ died for the sin of mankind" and "Christ died to save mankind." But the question remained as to how this was accomplished. Anselm addressed this question in his most memorable essay <u>Cur Deus Homo</u> (Why the God-man?).[24]

His answer to this question may also be summed up in a few phrases: "Make satisfaction for sin" and "Make atonement for sin."[25] He reasoned that the sin of humans created a debt owed to a righteous God. This debt had to be paid. This debt was satisfied by the blood sacrifice of the God-man. This solution to the problem has come to be called "the substitutionary atonement theory."

Some people argue the basic ideas were implicit in Paul's writings, the canonical gospels, the early church and the creeds. It is certainly possible to read Anselm's formulation back into those early materials, but this 11th-century scholastic theologian must be recognized as the one who enunciated the formula in the most logical way.

Anselm's work brought this doctrine to a central position in western Christianity. He was a priest and a practitioner of the rites of the church, but he went beyond the declaration of the efficacy of the rituals. "Substitutionary atonement," to be effective in providing salvation, required the faith of the parishioners. It is this union of the doctrine of salvation by substitutionary atonement with a necessary, particular kind of faith that was Anselm's contribution to theology in the 11th century. His legacy has lasted a thousand years and his theory is at the core of conservative Christianity today.

None of Anselm's rationale was at odds with the theology of the church and nothing really changed. The power of the church and the hierarchy was undiminished. The church was unchanged and Anselm took his place among the saints. But a seed was planted which had dramatic consequences for Christianity 600 years later in the subsequent cultural evolution of Christianity.

The hierarchical system with its monopoly of spiritual power lent itself to abuses. The power of the state deposited in the princes was a fierce power, but it paled in comparison to the eternal and ultimate power of the supernatural world, which the church hierarchy controlled. That mysterious terrifying supernatural world had its tentacles in every aspect of this world and all of human life. It was an ever-present, terrifying reality.

Hell, with its agonies, was real. Demons and angels roved both this world and the next. A just and vengeful God could wreak havoc in this world and administer the terrors of hell. Faced with these realities, what could the masses do but cower before the representatives of the supernatural world. These religious officials, who were both the conduits and administrators of supernatural power, often used it to their own benefit. They made personal and institutional demands with impunity and the system would brook no contradiction.

The Eastern Orthodox church, with its numerous national units, was a parallel hierarchical spiritual structure. The seat of authority and the central hierarchy was in Constantinople. There were national differences in symbolic, artistic representations and rituals, but the basic creeds and intellectual constructs were consistent with western Christendom. The general understanding of the supernatural world and the expected response to the mysteries of the unknown were essentially the same.

The medieval church received its first major challenge from the enlightenment and then from science. Scientists, as they gained in their power of explanation became ever more skeptical of traditional religious constructs relative to the physical world. Oppressive demands, endless spiritual terror, and the revelation of corrupt practices such as the sale of indulgences led to great unrest among the populace.

Exhausted by the physical and spiritual demands of the religious institution, the common man felt increasingly alienated and open to alternatives. Confidence in the religious hierarchy began to decline.

All this played into the hands of local priests and local social leaders who were closer to the people. These leaders, whether merely ambitious in their own interests or truly sympathetic with the people, challenged the upper levels of the hierarchy. The religious and social turmoil also played into the hands of secular princes who saw an opportunity to establish their regional power and exert control independent of the church. Thus the pope, archbishop and bishops lost their hold on many populations, particularly in northern Europe. Dislocation, in a system of social order, which had endured for more than a thousand years, was underway.

The religious hierarchy was successfully challenged and its power curbed. But what was to replace the church hierarchy and its religious power as the stabilizer of society? Martin Luther adopted a double approach. On the one hand he turned to the local princes with their political and military power. On the other hand he continued to rely on the mystifying and terrifying power of the spiritual world represented by the church.

The essentials of the creeds remained intact. In fact, as the hierarchy and its power declined, the importance of the Bible and its traditional interpretations increased. The merit of Christ's sacrifice had, in creedal and Anselmic thought, always functioned to purify and prepare souls for heaven. This was indeed the grace of God whereby all men must be saved. Access to heaven was a matter of "sola gracia" (grace alone). Luther made no reformulation of this crucial point.

But how was grace to flow from God in heaven to the people. The hierarchy and the church had done it for more than a millennium. How was grace to be administered now that the churchly hierarchy was gone? What was the conduit of grace to the people of this world. What was the mechanism by which grace was to be administered to the individual caught in the still fearsome and mystifying natural and supernatural worlds?

Luther provided a remarkable alternative.

He surely was acquainted with Anselm's essays. Here was a toehold for the reformation. For Luther, the Bible remained. But it was not the Bible itself or its complex conflicting set of messages which was the means of grace and its transmission.

Luther created a new authority and thereby a new conduit of grace. This creation was his central and critical doctrine of the reformation. "Sola fide," faith alone, was the means of grace. The individual in the church would receive the grace of God. One need only have faith.

But what is faith.[26] How does it work?

Luther retained all the basic elements of the creeds. All the fantastic, mysterious, miraculous supernatural ideas were still there. The merits and bounties of the atoning sacrifice of Christ was very much present. But now they were to be administered, not through a church hierarchy, but through a device called faith.

How did this faith function as the conduit of grace?

This faith, in its most elemental sense, is an intellectual assent to the creedal statements, the formulations of Anselm, and the complex supernatural world they envision. It is an affirmation of the creeds and doctrines as eternal truths. It is an absolute commitment to the perceived supernatural intervention as described in the doctrines. It is a confidence in the purported purposes of those interventions. These are all intellectual constructs.

Is the mental commitment to these intellectual constructs

sufficient to affect the flow of grace? Does it help to have a massive emotional component? One would receive the grace of God, one would be saved, one would go to heaven if one had this kind of faith. In the final analysis, in Luther's scheme of things, the reception and experience of the grace of God was a function of an adequate faith.

The burden to have this faith, this confidence in these supernatural events and their purposes devolved on the individual. No church, no hierarchy could assure an individual of the certainty of these matters. The individual had to do it alone.

"Sola fide" was the cornerstone of Luther's reformation. The hierarchical social structure of pope, archbishops, bishops and priests was gone, but the mysteries of the supernatural world remained.

Many rituals were retained, but modified and reformed. The populace went to church to corporately affirm their faith and thus receive the grace of God.

But this reformation left some awesome problems? What was the right kind of faith? When did one have enough faith to make the grace of God flow? Was faith an all or nothing thing? How much doubt could one have and still experience grace?

This was an age of doubt and questioning, scientific kinds of questioning. How could one know if one's faith was adequate? The uncertainty was an awful burden to bear.

John Calvin struggled with this issue and had an answer. His answer was clear. One could never know! Ultimately everything was in the hands of the all-powerful and all-knowing God. This was a tremendous relief. God would take care of everything. God would dispense the grace of human salvation purchased by the willing sacrifice of his own son and he would do this at his own whim and in his own good time. In some versions of Calvinist thought some people would be chosen and other people not. Some were damned by supernatural fiat and others were destined for heaven and the eternal experience of grace. Nothing anyone could do would change these realities.

The question of the sufficiency of faith was answered.

But every certain answer in this world seems to raise other questions. Calvin's answer might have been clear, but it was disconcerting. One's fate in the universe might be determined by election. But every human, in the moment after hearing Calvin's answer, awoke to a profound disease of the soul and a whimpering question.

Is there no hint of eternal destiny? Are there no evidences of election?

Scientific methodology was beginning to intrude into the religious world. Was there any data that could provide some hint of divine election or rejection? Surely if one was elected by God for eternal bliss there should be some foretaste, some indication of the eventual reward.

What, then, were the indications of grace? The grace of God would surely be accompanied by blessings in this life as well as the next. Comforts of life, approbation of one's fellows, power and prestige in the community surely were blessings. Since God is the source of all blessings, these material and social blessings surely were evidence of divine grace and precursors of greater blessings in heaven.

This formula was a profound relief for the elite in reformed society. Most people had to be satisfied with fewer and smaller evidences of election. Others had to live with the possibility of eternal damnation.

Apart from the removal of the hierarchy, its power to

administer grace and the elimination of churchly abuses – was any meaningful reformation accomplished? The fundamental elements of creedal Anselmic Christianity continued un-revised in the reformed churches and their multiple subdivisions in the past five centuries.

The most explicit expressions of this continuing mystery religion and the mechanisms of Anselmic faith are still found in virulent forms of American religious fundamentalism.

However, having made these critical observations of contemporary Christianity, one must recognize the continuing thread of Jesus' ethical work. It is a remarkably thin thread in many cases, but can be found. It can be found in the life of people who rise above their creeds or confessions and actually engage in works of redemptive love. Here, where the contemporary incarnation of Jesus is found, we will find him still doing his redemptive work and ethical teaching.

On occasion, throughout history, there were major efforts to recover the historical Jesus and implement his redemptive way of life. There were brotherhoods and communities, in which people attempted to live the life of Jesus. Most of these were declared heretical by the official church and often persecuted out of existence. One such attempt coincided in time with Luther and Calvin, and is known as the Anabaptist movement.

The culture in which this social movement developed was an amalgam of conflicting Catholic, Lutheran and Calvinist ideas – a culture where the general populace still perceived the supernatural world as the creeds described it.

The Anabaptists could not entirely escape the world in which they lived. But major modifications were made. Some creedal elements remained, but were significantly modified – their importance reduced and effectively pushed into the background. The commitment to the ethical teachings of Jesus became paramount.

For the Anabaptists, the Bible remained important and was an authoritative replacement for the hierarchical Christendom from which they came. But the message of the Bible was read selectively. The Sermon on the Mount, the ethical message of Paul's letters and the redemptive love in the life of Jesus became central elements in their thought. The dynamics of love were explicitly, deliberately, self-consciously brought to the fore in the context of a transformed theology and commitment to a transformed life.

For the Anabaptists, the love of one's fellowmen, membership in community, the sharing of goods and the sharing of one's human spirit were the practical essence of living out the message of Jesus. Faith in the potential of love to transform human life was the core commitment. This practical loving way of relationship enabled the merely human to evolve into the full social human being envisioned by the God of the universe. This redemptive capacity of Jesus' type of love reached even to one's enemies. This phenomenon was understood, in biblical language, as "growing into the stature of the fullness of Christ."

The Anabaptist branch of "Jesus Christianity" repudiates the core implications of modern American religious fundamentalism and its antecedents in the creeds, medieval Christianity, Anselm and the reformers. Anabaptism would claim that Constantinian Christianity is incapable of providing redemption for either individuals or society because it depends on magical supernaturalism.

"Jesus Christianity" is involved with practical love, the dynamic which provides forward movement in the evolution toward a full human being. It provides dynamic and motivation to "grow into the stature of the fullness of Christ."

# CHAPTER 8

# JESUS CHRISTIANITY AND CONSTANTINIAN CHRISTIANITY

The term "Christianity" is a clouded and confusing term open to contradictions and misunderstandings. It is used to refer to all kinds of different, even contradictory, ideas, behaviors, belief systems, attitudes, life-styles, behavior patterns, etc. It is even used to refer to certain institutional forms in contradistinction to other forms. Thus, in our confused world the term "Christian" is essentially meaningless. We should probably find other terms to describe the realities we experience in our different understandings of Jesus the Christ. To do so might enable us to grapple with fundamental issues in our discordant religious and social life.

However, for most people in Western culture, some nostalgic aura surrounds this term. Consequently, for this generation, it is probably an emotional impossibility to reject it. Furthermore, even though one might reject both the creeds of Christianity and the ethics of Jesus, it is socially dangerous to declare "I am not a Christian." Therefore, we will likely continue to use the term.

Given this reality it might be helpful to take a broader view of Christianity and recognize our confusion and the contradictions. This will require some courage. We might begin by admitting the existence of different forms of Christianity.

In the preceding material a number of terms have been used to describe different kinds of Christianity. Since this book is intended to describe a continuum, it will be useful to employ two terms to describe the extremes of this continuum.

The terms "Constantinian Christianity," "Creedal Christianity," Hellenic Christianity," "Anselmic Christianity," "American Fundamentalistic Christianity" and "Jesus Christianity" have appeared. It is time to clarify and differentiate these concepts.

The first five kinds of Christianity have most essential elements in common. Therefore, for the purposes of this chapter, they are all subsumed together in the most commonly used term "Constantinian Christianity," meaning creedal confessional Christianity.

"Jesus Christianity" has been defined in numerous, but consistent ways in the preceding chapters. It is my conclusion that "Jesus Christianity" has little in common with "Constantinian Christianity," but a great deal in common with the message and life of Jesus of the third decade of the CE.

These two types of Christianity may be polar opposites and thus have remarkably different consequences in the life of individuals and societies. In an academic sense they may be recognized as the extremes of a continuum, which attempts to accommodate the whole range of understandings of Christianity.

Let us try this with an attempt, in the first place, to characterize the kind of Christianity which is compatible with Jesus of Nazareth in Galilee and, secondly, the kind of Christianity compatible with the church fathers and the creeds at the time of Constantine in the fourth century.

The term "Christianity" rises from the term "Christ." The word "Christ" is the Greek translation of the Hebrew term Messiah, a term often translated as "anointed" or even better as "messenger."

Now, Jesus was in every sense a messenger. He delivered a profound ethical message to all mankind. A message about a creative response to the dilemmas of the human species. Jesus' message rejected violence and espoused love as the way to humanity's fuller evolution. For some people this was, and still is, a message of universal and eternal import. They perceive it as a message from the very essence of the universe. In this sense Jesus was a Christ. In this sense he was a "Christian."

For such people, Jesus was the Messiah, the Christ, the anointed one, the messenger. They justifiably define themselves as "Christian." But they reject the mystical, interpretations of Jesus' life and death, which lie at the core of the Constantinian kind of Christianity.

If those who espouse the magical mystical blood atonement type of salvation – the five-event religion – insist on calling themselves "Christian," then there are two kinds of Christianity and these two kinds are, in most points, diametrically opposed. There are then, it seems, two remarkably different kinds of Christianity. Therefore the designations "Jesus Christianity" and "Constantinian Christianity" seem useful.

Christianity in America is largely Constantinian Christianity. Jesus Christianity is little known and is offensive in American culture.

Contemporary Constantinian Christianity, in its many variations, traces elements of its belief and faith systems to creedal statements of the fourth and fifth centuries. The Christ of those documents had a message quite different from the message of Jesus. A message, in fact, at odds with Jesus in almost every respect.

The messenger of Constantinian Christianity is a miracle-working intruder from the supernatural world. This Christ is almost exclusively associated with five supernatural events purportedly attached to Jesus: the annunciation, miraculous virgin birth, crucifixion, resurrection, and ascension.

Constantinian Christianity contends these events are crucial to the means of salvation for the human race. They are, it is affirmed, the mechanisms by which we are saved from sin and eternal hell.

However, as we have seen in earlier chapters, these elements were common in the cultures of the Greco-Aramaic-Roman Near East. The cohabitation of a supernatural being with a human woman was not a strange idea. The idea of a God-man, a son of God, was present in ancient Persian, Chaldean and Hebrew thought and was very much a part of Greek mythology. The idea of sacrifice is consistent with the cultural practices of Greek, Roman and many other cultures as they sought to associate with the supernatural world.

The most important sacrifices in these cultures were instruments and devices to accomplish a relationship with the supernatural world and effect purification and escape from the consequences of sin. This was accomplished by the substitutionary blood sacrifice of animals and, in some cultures, human beings.

Making Christ the supreme ultimate atoning sacrifice is the most crucial element in current Constantinian Christianity. But this event is also the most transparent application of sacrifice for the expiation of sin found in ancient mystery religions.

Resurrection also was a common idea related to the transition from this world, or even from the underworld, to the supernatural world in Greek mythology and Egyptian religious thought.

These basic ideas underlay the belief systems of the medieval church. The same ideas, essentially unchanged, are still the core of much of contemporary Christianity. Present day mainline Christian denominations, and their fragmented derivative sub-denominations, still emphasize the same creedal statements and the five-event religion. The Greek and Roman mystery religion elements are even more sharply enunciated in contemporary fundamentalistic denominations.

Jesus was acquainted with these beliefs and knew them as elements of the Jewish, Greek and Roman culture in the region in which he lived. These religious ideas had been around for centuries. It was exactly these kinds of ideas that he rejected. Jesus would be appalled at a religion, which attaches him to these astounding magical-type myths.

At the core of Jesus' work lie two crucial interconnected messages. On the one hand, he proclaimed the good news of freedom from sacrificial practices and mysterious, mystical, magical beliefs. On the other, he proclaimed the good news of real redemption through the power of ethical human interrelationships.

As for Constantinian Christianity, there is only artificial forgiveness and magical salvation. The Constantinian message does not lead to ethical transformation or the redemptive experience of creative love. It does lead to the alienation of humans from their humanity. There is nothing either new or good in this message. There is no Gospel.

Constantinian Christianity and Jesus Christianity have vastly different purposes, and remarkably different outcomes. A summary might help us understand these differences.

Constantinian Christianity emphasizes life and actions of a supernatural world. Jesus Christianity emphasizes living in our natural world.

Constantinian Christianity calls us to reverence a supernatural world and its deities. Jesus Christianity calls us to reverence nature and our fellowmen.

Constantinian Christianity engages us with supernatural spirits. Jesus Christianity engages us with the spirit in our fellowmen.

Constantinian Christianity struggles to make humans into spiritual beings, something like gods. Jesus Christianity teaches us the true nature of humanity and opens our minds to human possibilities.

Constantinian Christianity teaches us to serve the gods in some symbolic, mystical spiritual way. Jesus Christianity teaches us to serve our fellow humans in practical, redemptive ways.

Constantinian Christianity pushes us to approach the supernatural with prayer and piety. Jesus Christianity pushes us to engage the real world with acts of love.

Constantinian Christianity expects us to live for a future world. Jesus Christianity expects us to live in and for this world.

Constantinian Christianity exalts us above creation. It sacralizes the domination and violation of creation. Jesus Christianity places us in creation: We are not above it, we are not superior to it, we are a part of it.

Constantinian Christianity would have us believe in miracles, the violation of natural law. Jesus Christianity calls us to be free within the realm of natural laws.

Constantinian Christianity makes fear of the supernatural world a tool to control people. Jesus Christianity rejects fear and espouses love as the means of influencing people.

Constantinian Christianity teaches the superiority of the supernatural and the inferiority of the natural world. Jesus Christianity teaches us the primary importance of this world where we can grow into human beings unhindered by supernatural beings.

Constantinian Christianity proclaims human nothingness and powerlessness. Jesus Christianity shows us the way to be powerful creators of our fellowmen.

Constantinian Christianity sets us in awe of supernatural powers. Jesus Christianity opens the way to feel the pain of the weak.

Constantinian Christianity sacralizes violence as the means of control.[27] Jesus Christianity sacralizes love as the means to reconciliation.

Constantinian Christianity asks us to labor for the supernatural world. Jesus Christianity asks us to work for this world and our fellowmen.

Constantinian Christianity has reduced humans to sinners. Jesus Christianity enables humans to overcome sin.

Constantinian Christianity forces us to deny our humanity. Jesus Christianity permits us to realize the potential of our humanity.

Constantinian Christianity is a mystery religion. It is a mechanism, which divorces us from our world and the human race. It creates fear and makes escape dependent on fantastic magical manipulations of unknown spirits in an unknowable world. Jesus Christianity rejects all such nonsense.

It is surely time for all of Christianity to join Jesus and the human race.

## CHAPTER 9

# THEOLOGY AND LIFE

In the preceding chapters sharp distinctions have been made between Constantinian, or fundamentalistic, Christianity and the kind of Christianity that reflects the life practiced and advocated by Jesus. Theoretically the distinction may be clear. However, few people other than academics are concerned about Christianity in a theoretical sense.

What really matters is the life of people who call themselves Christian.

Certainly the mental constructs we carry about in our minds – our beliefs – do matter. Ideas have consequences and implications for life. But they are not the whole of life; often they are a very small part of life. In the final analysis the way we interact with our fellow human beings is crucial. The way we relate to those we love and those we tend not to love, even to those who are enemies, is important.

There are people who give mental assent to the doctrines, dogmas and confessions of faith, which are promulgated as absolute truths by their churches. They may have an intellectual conviction about the ultimate veracity of the doctrines. They may have some emotional attachment to them. But many of these people, despite such convictions, know there is more to human realities than a complex of ideas and emotions.

Some of these people live a life of love, a life which has redemptive consequence. They are aware that relationships are important, maybe even more important than any intellectual or emotional construct. To interact with such people leaves one more whole and free, more human.

But, there are also people who reject religious doctrines and most assuredly reject the Constantinian, creedal constructs of Christianity. They make no appeal to a supernatural world. Many of these live a life of care, concern and forgiveness. They live a life of love, which has redemptive, re-creative consequences. To interact with these people makes one more whole and free, more human, more able to live and love.

Is it possible there is no correlation between belief systems and the interactive, redemptive quality of life?

Although there may be no necessary connection between ideology and the redemptive quality of life, the question still remains: Do ideologies affect life? Do they influence or even determine the way we act and interact with people far and near?

Before grappling with this question, it may be of interest to encounter the idea of "truth." What is truth? The question has been asked before.

The term is generally associated with a concept, which becomes a fact when it is shown to be related to reality. Science has had some success in finding facts. A scientifically-supported fact is generally understood to be a "truth," at least in a scientifically-oriented world.

Imagination, on the other hand, has been singularly ineffective in finding facts and a total failure in finding "truth." But imagination has been marvelously successful in producing beliefs. This is particularly evident in the realm of the unknowable[28] where revelation seems so active. In no way should "beliefs" or "revelations" be confused with facts, and most assuredly they should not be equated with truth.

When people confuse belief with fact they do not have "truth." What they have is an ideology. Belief systems are always ideologies. Ideologues inevitably declare their beliefs to be "truth." Beliefs exist, ideologies exist, but neither fact nor truth are necessarily present.

Religion is remarkably prone to the production of ideologies. Any religious person confirms this in the normal process of condemning other religious beliefs as "false," "pagan," "demonic," "unGodly," or even just an "ideology." The ideologue rejects alternate ideas and may even reject human beings who hold alternate ideas. This is marvelously injurious and devastating to the human race.

Is there some way for human beings to escape this trap?

It has been the burden of this book to suggest that religion can have an ethical dimension. If this is true, and the belief component of religion is only ideological, we may have to find truth in ethical living. Here we may be on solid ground. Relationships that generate and create whole human beings seem to be "truth" if we look at the data and a vast body of scientific work.

It is intriguing to refer to Jesus in this context. He is reported to have made people free from all kinds of debilitating conditions and relationships. He did it by relating to them in many different ways, all of them redemptive. In so doing he enabled them to be more whole, more free, more human. The beginning point of his approach to the truth of relationship was the rejection of dogma, tradition and ideology. He got into serious trouble with the religious authorities because he refused to place doctrine, dogma and ideology above relationships. In fact, he was killed essentially because he rejected the exclusive and restrictive ideology of both the religious and political authorities of his day.

Truth, for Jesus, was relational not ideological. Jesus' kind of truth is truth that makes the human being free. Truth lies in the processes of redemptive, creative relationships, not in dogmas, doctrines, creeds, or any mental constructs, which claim to have a grip on the unknowable universe. Most assuredly, in Jesus Christianity truth is a process, not an intellectual construct.

It is the processes of creative relationships that we must practice in order to have truth. This is possible regardless of belief.

But surely this kind of interrelationship is more likely if the human is aware that the dogmas of ideologies are irrelevant to the real work of redemption and salvation. These processes of salvation and redemption exist not because of ideologies, but in spite of ideologies.

All humans do have beliefs and ideologies. Where one finds an ideological commitment to revelations and beliefs about the unknowable world, it is likely the importance of relationship with people in our human world will be minimized.

In such circumstances, ideologically-held creeds, confessions, doctrines and dogmas function as instruments of exclusion and rejection. Such behavior results in human devaluation, violence and, ultimately, individual and social degeneration.[29]

However, if one has an ideology which affirms that creative, redemptive relationships are paramount and supercede all other beliefs, surely the processes of creation will more likely be practiced and redemption more likely accomplished. In the context of these realities, human beings will "grow into the stature of the fullness of Christ."

This is the kind of truth that will make us free!

# APPENDICES

# SOCIAL SCIENCE LOOKS AT RELIGION

How does one explain the tremendous variation in descriptions of the supernatural world? How does one explain the acrimonious debate about God from culture to culture, and within western Christian society from denomination to denomination? How does one account for the contradictions we find in the definition of God from person to person even within denominations? Is it purely a matter of ignorance or special insight.

Why is religion a taboo subject in good company? Why does this subject inspire anxiety and hostility when contrary ideas are encountered?

Our five senses or their instrumental extensions provide us with everything we know about the universe. Neither the senses nor their extensions have been able to detect, much less describe, anything of a supernatural world. Obviously then, the supernatural world must fall into the category of the unknowable. In any scientific sense it is impossible to know the unknowable.

Not withstanding this scientific reality, the world seems to be full of people who claim to know much about a supernatural world. They claim the supernatural world has power, even different forms of power. These powers may take spiritual form. Some people personalize these powers and spirits and refer to them as deities or gods. Many people, with great passion and certainty, describe the attributes and characteristics of their God or gods.

These same people claim the supernatural world can intrude into this natural world. While here these deities do all kinds of things, even things that violate the known laws of nature. Some people believe the deities can interact with human beings and are able to influence events for good or ill. They claim the deities can bring messages from the supernatural world to the human world.

Moreover many, particularly in Hellenistic religions and Constantinian Christianity, have observed the gods in human form and have detected characteristics similar to humans. According to these testimonials, the gods love and hate, they take sides in quarrels, they favor humans who serve them and punish humans who don't. They also have the ability to move between the supernatural and natural realms.

Many people claim to know some of these deities. They know their names. They know their characteristics and what they can do in this world. They fear the demons of that supernatural world and fear them even more when they intrude into this world. Many people claim intimacy with the most powerful and beneficent. Some who claim intimacy with these beneficent powers and deities also claim marvelous benefits, benefits which in the most dramatic sense will save them from the company of malevolent deities in an eternal hell and transport them to heaven and eternal bliss.

Humans have been making these claims and similar ones from the beginning of time. The testimonials relative to these matters differ from claimant to claimant, from time to time, from place to place. The descriptions of human experiences with these powers and deities are sometimes contradictory and even diametrically opposed.

How is all this possible? No scientist, or any human for that matter, has ever yet found a way to test these claims. Since this is the case, any claims relative to the supernatural must remain hypothetical. We have absolutely no evidence relative to the supernatural world.

However, we do have a vast set of data relative to what individuals and groups think and believe about the supernatural world and the powers present there.

Now it should be clear that what people believe about the supernatural world and what is real in the universe do not necessarily coincide. The human mind is capable of imagining and fabricating all kinds of mental constructs the referents of which cannot be detected by any known means. Human ideas are one thing. The reality of the supernatural realm and its characteristics are something entirely different and, by definition, unknowable.

How then is it possible for many humans to feel they have certain knowledge of the unknowable? This is a marvelous conundrum. Is it possible that humans actually know nothing about the supernatural but only think they know? We have massive amounts of data relative to this question and can easily gather more.

Just ask a stranger to describe the supernatural. That person will likely be able to give you some information. However, if that person's view differs from another person's view, is that clear evidence that they know nothing of the supernatural? Is it possible that both are mistaken and know nothing.

Testimony uttered in a calm, hushed, pious, or raucous

desperate declaration reflects only an individualistic conviction of certainty, nothing more.

Maybe the supernatural world, the unknown world really, in the final analysis, is unknowable! A scientist would declare this to be truth. A scientist will admit to a total ignorance of the unknowable.

And yet there is an almost universal affirmation among many people in most societies that a supernatural world exists.

It is obvious then, if we are to understand the supernatural world and learn of its source we must search elsewhere than in a supernatural world or the testimonials of believers.

Anthropological and sociological disciplines have been engaged in this search with some measure of success.

In traditional religion it is assumed the supernatural world and its powers created this world and everything in it. Most crucially, it is believed, the gods inspire the mores of social interaction and the approved forms of institutions by which societies maintain themselves. Multitudes of people believe in supernatural powers. They believe the gods called their society into existence. Moreover they believe their society is sacred because the gods made it.

Is this really the causal connection? Is it possible the opposite might be true?

Anthropological studies have noted the similarities between the powers and organizational characteristics of societies and the ways in which people of those societies understand the characteristics and organizational patterns of their supernatural world. These parallels are not accidental. The models which imagination uses to construct the supernatural are always the familiar. The way the powers and spiritual beings interact in the supernatural world is always similar to the way human organization is experienced in this world.

The interaction patterns and institutional forms in the real social world are the raw materials used to construct the supernatural world. The social patterns in this world are idealized and then projected into the supernatural world. Inevitably and logically, the gods and supernatural forces are only reflections of a society's social world.

The idealized supernatural world has no real substance in any rational scientific sense. But it is real to the believers.

They believe in the reality of its manifold powers. By faith they believe the supernatural world is capable of communicating with them. The message the humans receive from their God or gods is always identical to their own view of the world. The supernatural world thus, inevitably and predictably, approves, endorses, and sacralizes the culture which created it.

The process by which the supernatural world is constructed by modern society is no different than the processes by which tribal societies of the past have constructed their supernatural worlds. National groups are essentially tribal groups and if we are to understand contemporary societies, and such things as patriotism and war, we must apply the same procedures of analysis that have been so useful in understanding the religions of tribal societies.

Tribal groups needed explanations of their origins. They needed justification for their existence and legitimation of their social structures. They needed affirmation of their identity and worth, over against all others. They needed a consciousness of their place in the order of things in this world. They needed help in the awesome challenges of existence in a mysterious physical and troubling social world.

Where does one turn for help with all these human dilemmas? The answers are not easy to find in this world.

Under such circumstances it is convenient and comfortable to turn to the supernatural world. The answers from that world are always absolute and incontrovertible, and always consistent with the values of the society or groups within society.

The perceived reality of the supernatural world guides and controls. It provides a model for the society's forms and patterns of order.

In summary, it must be clear that societies and the supernatural create and modify each other in reciprocal ways.

The powers, spirits, beings, deities, gods, devils and other powers of the supernatural world differ from society to society just as societies differ from one another.

Supernatural powers are always viewed as more powerful than earthly powers and they are powerful in many different ways. Each God has special characteristics and is responsible for specific activities in this world. Sometimes the deities work together, at other times they work in opposition. The supernatural world is confusing just as the natural world is confusing.

Since this world is terrifying, one finds the supernatural world to be terrifying. Powers of all kinds abound in this world, therefore also in the supernatural world. A cyclical interaction occurs. As the gods quarrel, the nation-states quarrel; and as the nation-states quarrel, the gods quarrel – and on and on. Violence begets violence, hate begets hate. Turmoil and tragedy become the lot of humans caught in the maelstrom of this circular interaction between their world and the fantastic spiritual world.

There are, then, as many forms of deities as there are social groups. Polytheistic societies perceive numerous powers in their supernatural world. Each of the gods has its own character, power and function. Those societies affirming monotheism tend to see their single deity with multiple characteristics, forms or modes. In Constantinian Christianity there are at least three modes of expression: Father, Son and Holy Spirit. The creeds attempt to differentiate these modes. The debates and confusions about the differences continue unabated to this day with disastrous consequences.

The different modes of the monotheistic gods of Constantinian Christian, Muslim and Jewish cultures function in the same ways as different gods in a polytheistic supernatural world.

Some monotheistic traditions do not really claim a single God, but they do claim the superiority of their own God.

The supposed advance of Hebrew monotheism developed in the context of inter-societal conflict. The Israelites found themselves enslaved by Egyptian pharaohs and struggled toward freedom. They had a traditional tribal God Yahweh, a God different and distinct from the Egyptian gods. The Israelites saw their struggle as the struggle of deities. Their escape from slavery in Egypt, and their ultimate successful passage through lands of alien people, was adequate proof of Yahweh's superiority. He was clearly a God above all gods. There is no notion that the God of Abraham, Isaac and Jacob was the only God, he was only a superior God.

If the gods could be defeated, the aliens and enemies could be defeated. If the society could defeat alien societies, the God of the successful society would be enabled to defeat the God of the alien society. The reciprocal relationship between societies and their gods is obvious. In the face of danger a society will serve its gods and, it is assumed, the gods will respond with societal prosperity.

But this is always problematic. Sometimes the gods fail to

deliver. If a society's gods fail, individual and societal disillusionment and disintegration occurs. The society, then, dissolves or changes dramatically and extensively.

Societies are fractured, and people are set over against one another in this real social world. The liberal notion that we are all worshipping the same God is no solution because the deities still act independently and aggressively against each other in their reincarnation in the societies which created them.

What, in summary, does one find in the supernatural world?

We find exactly what each society has put there. The supernatural world is the idealized projection of one's own culture and nothing more.

The fact that many people believe in the existence of a supernatural world is incontrovertibly proven by science. There is abundant evidence that multitudes of people believe in the existence of deities, spirits and gods.

But there is no evidence that such a world exists. There is no evidence that supernatural powers exist. These things do not exist in reality, but they do exist in fantasies. And these fantasies have real consequences. It is these fantasies and their consequences that are the real social realities.

To understand all this is the beginning of knowledge.

## APPENDIX B

# SOME CREEDS OF THE EARLY CHRISTIAN CHURCH

Most Christian groups and denominations trace their belief systems to the creeds of the early church. Most presume a continuity from the New Testament. Four of the most common and well-known creeds are reproduced below and a reading will provide an opportunity to think about the ways in which one's own belief system accords with the belief system of the church fathers. There are many other copies and versions of these early church creeds. You may find them as supplemental materials in hymn books and other liturgical sources.

## THE APOSTLES CREED

I believe in God, the Father almighty, Creator of heaven and earth. I believe in Jesus Christ, His only Son, our Lord. He was conceived by the power of the Holy Spirit, and born of the Virgin Mary. He suffered under Pontius Pilate, was crucified, died and buried. He descended to the dead. On the third day He rose again. He ascended into heaven, and is seated at the right hand of the Father. He will come again to judge the living and the dead. I believe in the Holy Spirit, the holy Catholic Church, the communion of saints, the forgiveness of sins, the resurrection of the body, and the life everlasting. Amen.

# THE NICENE CREED, 325 CE

We believe in one God, the Father Almighty, Maker of heaven and earth, and of all things visible and invisible. And in one Lord Jesus Christ, the only-begotten Son of God, begotten of the Father before all worlds, God of God, Light of Light, Very God of Very God, begotten, not made, being of one substance with the Father, by Whom all things were made; Who for us men, and for our salvation, came down from heaven, and was incarnate by the Holy Spirit of the Virgin Mary, and was made man, and was crucified also for us under Pontius Pilate. He suffered and was buried, and the third day He rose again according to the Scriptures, and ascended into heaven, and sits on the right hand of the Father. And He shall come again with glory to judge both the quick and the dead, Whose kingdom shall have no end. And we believe in the Holy Spirit, the Lord and Giver of Life, Who proceeds from the Father and the Son, Who with the Father and the Son together is worshipped and glorified, Who spoke by the prophets. And we believe one holy catholic and apostolic church. We acknowledge one baptism for the remission of sins. And we look for the resurrection of the dead, and the life of the world to come. Amen.

# CREED OF CHALCEDON, 451 CE

Following the holy fathers, therefore, we all with one accord teach the profession of faith in the one identical Son, our Lord Jesus Christ. We declare that He is perfect both in His divinity and in His humanity, truly God and truly man, composed of body and rational soul, that He is consubstantial with the Father in His Divinity, and consubstantial with us in His humanity, like us in every respect except for sin. We declare that in His Divinity, He was begotten of the Father before time, and in His humanity He was begotten in this last age of Mary, the virgin, the mother of God*, for us and our salvation. We declare that the one selfsame Christ, only begotten Son and Lord, must be acknowledged in two natures, without any co-mingling, or change or division or separation, that the distinction between their natures is in no way removed by their union, but rather, that the specific character of each nature is preserved, and they are united in one person and one hypostasis. We declare that He is not split nor divided into two persons, but that there is one, selfsame, only-begotten Son, God the Word, the Lord Jesus Christ. This, the prophets have taught about Him from the beginning; this, Jesus Christ Himself taught us; this, the Creed of the Fathers has handed down to us. *(Note: Theotokos, also translated "God-bearer".)

## CREED OF ATHENASIUS

### Trinitarian Formulation

Whoever wishes to be saved must, above all, keep the catholic faith. For unless a person keeps this faith whole and entire he will undoubtedly be lost forever.

This is what the catholic faith teaches.

We worship one God in the Trinity and the Trinity in unity. We distinguish among the persons, but we do not divide the substance. For the Father is a distinct person; the Son is a distinct person; and the Holy Spirit is a distinct person. Still the Father and the Son and the Holy Spirit have one divinity, equal glory, and co-eternal majesty. What the Father is, the Son is, and the Holy Spirit is. The Father is uncreated, the Son is uncreated, and the Holy Spirit is uncreated. The Father is boundless, the Son is boundless, and the Holy Spirit is boundless. The Father is eternal, the Son is eternal, and the Holy Spirit is eternal. Nevertheless, there are not three eternal beings, but one eternal being. Thus there are not three uncreated beings, nor three boundless beings, but one uncreated being and one boundless being. Likewise, the Father is omnipotent, the Son is omnipotent, and the Holy Spirit is omnipotent. Yet there are not three omnipotent beings, but one omnipotent being. Thus the Father is God, the Son is God, and the Holy Spirit is God. But there are not three gods, but one God. The Father is Lord, the Son is Lord, and the Holy Spirit is Lord. There are not three lords, but one Lord. For according to Christian truth, we must profess that each of the persons individually is God; and according to Christian religion we are forbidden to say that there are three gods or lords. The Father is not made by anyone, nor created by anyone, nor generated by anyone. The Son is not made nor created, but he is generated by the Father alone. The Holy Spirit is not made nor created nor generated, but proceeds from the Father and the Son. There is, then, one Father, not three Fathers; one Son, but not three sons; one Holy Spirit, not three holy spirits. In this Trinity, there is nothing greater, nothing less than anything else. But the entire three persons are co-eternal and coequal with one another. So that, as we have said, we worship complete unity in the Trinity and the Trinity in unity.

This, then, is what he who wishes to be saved must believe about the Trinity.

It is also necessary for eternal salvation that he believes steadfastly in the incarnation of our Lord Jesus Christ. The true faith is: we believe and profess that our Lord Jesus Christ, the Son of God, is both God and man. As God He was begotten of the substance of the Father before time; as man He was born in time of the substance of His Mother. He is perfect God; and He is perfect man, with a rational soul and human flesh. He is equal to the Father in His divinity, but He is inferior to the Father in His humanity. Although He is God and man, He is not two, but one Christ. And He is one, not because His divinity was changed into flesh, but because His humanity was assumed to God. He is one, not at all because of a mingling of substances, but because He is one person. As a rational soul and flesh are one man: so God and man are one Christ. He died for our salvation, descended to hell, arose from the dead on the third day. Ascended into heaven, sits at the right hand of God the Father almighty, and from there He shall come to judge the living and the dead. At His coming, all men are to arise with their own bodies; and they are to give an account of their lives. Those who have done good deeds will go into eternal life; those who have done evil will go into everlasting fire.

This is the Catholic faith. Everyone must believe it, firmly and steadfastly; otherwise He cannot be saved. Amen

*APPENDIX C*

# RELIGION AND SOCIAL ORDER

Sociology of Religion is a standard course of study in any sociology curriculum. The following essay draws on years of teaching this course at the college senior level.

The essay uses sociological principles to address the following topics: **I.** Differentiating customary ordered behavior and ethical ordered behavior; **II.** Ways in which religion might be associated with each of these two categories; **III.** What happens when the expected behavior in each category is violated; **IV.** Proposed mechanisms to restore order; **V.** The key needed to activate the mechanisms designed to restore order for societies and all human beings.

## I. Two types of behavior: Customary and Ethical

Order in any society is critical for stability and survival.

Every society must have general agreements about beliefs, practices and behaviors, or chaos will occur. People in a society must know what to expect from other people. These predictable behaviors are known as customs. In general they are so ingrained that we are unaware of them until there is a violation.

Behaviors are not all of the same importance.

Passing left shoulder to left shoulder as we approach another person on the sidewalk is expected. This is an example of a "folkway." It is a behavior that is customary, but hardly crucial for the survival of a society.

Fidelity in marriage is considered foundational to the stability of family. Fidelity is a "more" and its violation an "immoral" behavior. Infidelity does occur and causes disruption for the immediate social group, but the society as a whole does not disintegrate.

However, driving on the right or left side of the road is a serious matter. If this behavior were unpredictable the consequences would be serious. Morgues would do a thriving business. Traffic would come to an end. Commerce would collapse. Our society as we know it would disintegrate. There are numerous other behaviors that, if practiced widely, would destroy society in its basic formulation. Societies try to preserve their integrity by establishing "laws" and legal systems to punish violators of crucial and essential behaviors.

In summary: "Folkways" are of minimal importance; "mores" are more crucial to the integrity of a society; "laws" relate to behaviors which are absolutely essential for the maintenance of a society.

All of these vary from society to society, time to time, place to place and circumstance to circumstance. Appropriate attire varies from America to Armenia, 1890 to 1990, formal dining to beachside picnic. Even the most serious behavior – murder – prohibited by law in every society, becomes moral and legal if the state defines the person as an enemy. Under conditions of warfare it is moral to kill and even immoral not to kill.

Clearly, there is nothing either absolute or universal about customary behaviors. They depend entirely on the particular culture at a particular time. What is customary in "folkways," "mores," and "laws" is simply a matter of societal consensus or the dictates of the powerful.

Ethical behavior, on the other hand, differs qualitatively from customary behavior. Ethical behavior is concerned with all humanity and the entire realm of human existence. It encompasses all behaviors that produce universal stability and order.

Here we are concerned not only with individual behaviors, as they affect all other humans, but also with the behavior of larger social bodies: organizations, institutions and whole societies. What forms of politics, family, education, economics and other institutions will maximize the humanness of all humanity? What kind of societal interaction will provide for stability and security for all societies and all their citizens? What behaviors will lead to the greatest good for all humanity and the earth itself? These are the ethical questions.

Ethical behavior maximizes the positive effects of relationships between human beings and all dimensions of their social and physical world. The discipline of ethics searches for ultimate universal standards of behavior.

How are these two categories of behavior – customary behavior and ethical behavior – related to religion?

## II. Religion and Types of Behavior

Every society assumes its forms of institutions are superior to all others. Societies attempt to validate their customs by reference to fundamental principles or supernatural dimensions or both. To the extent that there is an appeal to the supernatural world and its spirits, deities, entities or principles, religion is present.

What is immediately obvious is that societies have different supernatural worlds.[30] Each society appeals to its own supernatural world for validation of its own system of customary behavior. This sacralization of institutional forms by a society, leads inevitably to isolation from and conflict with other societies. It results in the demonization of alternate institutional forms and the dehumanization of people in other societies.

Ethical concerns look beyond the local definition of what is good and right. Ethics look beyond local assumptions and their supporting deities, to the universal good.

Ethics analyze the way particular institutional forms and particular societies work for the good or ill of all human beings. In a religious perspective, ethical behavior assumes a supernatural world beyond the national, tribal or individualistic supernatural worlds. From this perspective, ethical behavior assumes a supernatural world or a realm of principles where universal principles, not local customs, are the guides for all behaviors.

It is obvious that customary behaviors are, in fact, frequently in violation of ethical standards. Customary behaviors are concerned with local, societal behaviors. Often these are selfish, and consider only the local good. Consequently, customary behaviors may be and often are violations of standards of ethical behavior.

In the real world, customary and ethical behaviors are often in contradiction. These contradictions produce confusion and provoke intense debate in all societies.

In the real world, violations of both customary behavior and ethical behavior do occur.

Disorder ensues, sin occurs.

## III. Disorder

## A. Uncustomary Behavior

Let us discuss, first, uncustomary behavior in the context of national societies.

Two millennia ago, in Greek city-states, the city fathers concerned themselves with ordered behaviors. They made and enforced laws to maintain civic order without appeal to the supernatural world. But, for most people in Jewish, Greek and Roman cultures, customary behaviors were the concern of societal deities and their supernatural world. If customs were violated, turmoil occurred in both the human social world and the supernatural world. Disorder and sin were present. Modern societies are no different in any of these respects.

"Sin" is a religious word, but it means essentially the same thing as "disorder." If one is religious in the Constantinian sense, "sin" may seem more appropriate. If one is religious in the Jesus sense, either word is appropriate. If one is avowedly non-religious, "disorder" may seem more acceptable. Let us use them interchangeably to describe any conditions of destructive interaction experienced by humans in their contacts with the social, physical or supernatural worlds.

The more extensive the intrusion of the supernatural world into a given society[31] the more comprehensive is the catalogue of sins. It follows logically that sin differs from God to God, society to society, place to place and time to time. In nonreligious societies a catalogue of disorders also exists.

However, social change does occur and the "sin" and "disorder" catalogues are frequently revised.

Western Christian societies have made revisions with

considerable ease. A short list of such changes might include divorce, serial marriage, premarital sex, abortion, homosexual behavior, war, capital punishment etc. Obviously, the gods change their minds as people change their minds.[32]

In religious traditions, in addition to societal customs there are human-supernatural interactions. There are correct beliefs, correct rituals, correct attitudes, correct sacrifices, correct services, correct thoughts and correct emotional responses. These are ordinarily prescribed and elaborated in the creeds, confessions of faith, prayer books, orders of service and informal customs. These constitute the mechanisms of relationship with the supernatural world.

In less religious societies, or even avowedly nonreligious societies, traditions and rituals play the same role. All societies have ideologies and ideals that demand customary behaviors, moods and emotions, which become routinized and are crucial to societal identity.

Improper behavior, improper beliefs and improper observance of societal customs and rituals produce sin and disorder. It is sin to have thoughts that might offend the supernatural. It is sin to act in ways that are not customary to the normal pattern of things in a national society. This is evident in the American national religion where the American God, the American psyche, is easily offended by activities designated as unpatriotic.

## B. Unethical Behavior

In the context of an ethical worldview, the catalogue of disorder and sin is markedly different. Unethical behavior, sin and disorder occur where the fundamental laws of constructive human relations are violated. We sin when we act in ways that diminish the humanity of any other group or individual. We sin against the universal social world when we act in selfish ways that benefit our own society to the disadvantage of other societies and peoples. A short list would surely include: discrimination, war, exploitation and monopolistic control of resources.

How we interact with the physical world is also an ethical issue. Those concerned with sustainable societies have a catalogue of relevant unethical activities. A short list would surely include: overpopulation, pollution, degradation of the earth. Surely, anything that threatens the intricate web of life is sin. To think and act independently of all of life, and everything on which life depends, is unethical.

Ethical behavior is the essence of Jesus Christianity. In this kind of Christianity, sin and disorder appear in disruptive, exploitive relationships with one's fellowmen and the physical world on which we all depend. Jesus was not concerned with the sanctity of local folkways, mores and laws. He was concerned with ethical behavior, which is positive for all humans.

At this juncture of history we seem to be living in a disordered world. The consequences are devastating to both humans and the physical world itself. Is there no escape? Can nothing be done about disorder, sin or unethical behavior?

To summarize, there are two distinct categories of behavior: customary behavior and ethical behavior. Sometimes they are in contradiction.

In the real world, violations of both kinds of behavior occur. What is to be done if violations occur? What is to be done if customs are violated? Is it possible to live without sin and disorder? What can be done if unethical behaviors occur? Is there a way to live ethically? Is there a way to restore order to the world?

## IV. Mechanisms for the Restoration of Order

Both Constantinian Christianity and Jesus Christianity propose solutions to the problem of disorder and sin. Both kinds of Christianity have formulas for salvation. But they differ markedly in their definition of disorder and differ irreconcilably in the solution.

From the perspective of Constantinian Christianity, sin and disorder are inextricably intertwined with the supernatural world. Since the church is the institution dealing with the unknown supernatural world, the church is intimately concerned with definitions of sin. Religion and churches are obsessed with their own particular catalogue of sins and have elaborate systems of salvation. Is it possible that sin is their very reason for being?

In Constantinian Christianity, salvation from sin is dependent on the restoration of order with the supernatural world. Humans in respect to this perceived reality are powerless. Salvation is a task for the gods and must be accomplished according to their formulas.

Since time immemorial, human societies have understood these formulas to entail services to deities and spirits in the form of sacrifices and rituals of various kinds. If these are performed correctly, the supernatural world blesses the society with security, health, food and stable social relations. If the services are inadequate, human life becomes chaotic and problematic. The world beyond waits ready with even more horrendous endless terrors.

To escape sin and its consequences, ordered relationships must be reestablished by proper, powerful services and sacrifices. Constantinian Christianity takes care of sin and restores order in a remarkably dynamic way. God himself, at Calvary, performed the perfect sacrifice with the perfect victim – his own son. This is the mechanism that placates the just and angry God, removes the offense of sin and restores the human to supernatural favor. Through this device – the sacrifice of "Christ" – humans bypass all the terrible consequences of sin.

This mechanism was the central concern of the medieval church and continues to be an obsession with its current incarnation in Christian fundamentalism. In this formula, nothing is said about the real and enduring effects of sin or the way in which real and enduring order is to be restored to the domain of human relations and the conditions of the earth.

In Constantinian Christianity, the formula for restoring order is designed by God. However, it is not automatic. The human must respond. The human must turn the key to activate the mechanism of salvation. That key is "faith."

Jesus Christianity has a different approach to the problem of disorder and unethical behavior. In Jesus Christianity, sin is a reality in this world and must be dealt with here – not in some supernatural world. Jesus rejected sacrifice as a mechanism to deal with sin. Blood sacrifices were no more effective than any other. The only sacrifice that meets approval in Jesus Christianity is the giving up of selfishness, power and exploitative control.

The solution, the cure for sin, is not some miraculous, mystical, ritualistic washing. The cure for sin, according to Jesus, is to stop sinning. "Go and sin no more" was the core of his teaching about sin. "Love your fellowmen" was the mechanism that redeemed both the offender and the offended.

There is nothing mysterious, miraculous, supernatural, fantastic or magical in Jesus' solution to sin. Sin is taken realistically and seriously. Repentance occurs by restoring right relationship with both the natural world and its human inhabitants. It is a matter of loving one's fellowmen and the earth on which we live.

Jesus Christianity resonates with ethical behavior, common sense, logical thought and scientific knowledge. If we are to heal the hurts of the earth, we must stop hurting it. If we are to undo alienation from our fellowmen, we must stop treating them violently and begin to love them and restore relationships.

How do those who believe Jesus' formula for salvation activate its processes? The key is "faith."

Constantinian and Jesus Christians agree: Faith is the key.

## V. The Key to the Restoration of Order

But what is faith? It might be helpful to repeat a simple definition.

Faith is a mental and emotional behavior. It is an intellectual commitment to a perceived truth. It is an affirmation of propositions that the faithful hold as ultimately valid. It is a sense of certainty that one has insight and knowledge above and beyond all others. Finally, it is action – a whole range of behaviors, which express in practical ways the commitments to the propositions and the principles that flow from them.

It is a confidence that the formula to deal with sin is true, will work and has abiding consequences. There is a certain conviction that one has truth despite the lack of evidence for either propositions or formulas.

Faith has little concern with scientific data. It exists regardless of proof or the lack of proof. This is true for both types of Christianity. But the similarity ends there. The propositions and formulas that are the objects of faith are vastly different.

How does faith act in Constantinian Christianity?

What is critical here is a certainty about the supernatural world: Its nature; its extension into this world; its power to do things. Lack of scientific data is no hindrance to faith.

There is no scientific data supporting the idea of a supernatural world, but faith has framed it and described its powers. There is no evidence of virgin births. Hence a virgin birth is a product of faith. There is no evidence that a God can become human. Thus, to believe that Jesus was the earthly incarnation of a monotheistic God takes faith. There is no proof the bloodletting of either God or man will atone for sin or restore order to anything. Therefore a belief in absolution by the crucifixion of a particular God-man takes faith. There is no scientific evidence of a physical resurrection of a dead body. But faith can accomplish this feat. The data for the ascension of a body to the supernatural world is completely lacking. But faith, for the true believer, can make all of these into a kind of reality.

Faith defies evidence. Faith defies doubt. Faith makes the creeds dynamic and persistent. Faith has consequences in the real world.

But is this kind of faith redemptive? Does it really take care of sin? Does the glorified violence at Calvary or any other place restore order? Are its consequences ethical?

In the final analysis, Constantinian Christianity makes the supernatural world primary. The world in which we live is essentially irrelevant. All is purely a matter between a man and his God. God can do everything and will do everything. This creed releases the human being from responsibility for other human beings, any social group or the world itself.

In this formula, God takes care of all sin by a miraculous

blood sacrifice of the God-man 2,000 years ago. Since sin is expunged by this supernatural violent mechanism, human social responsibility disappears. In this magical system of sin and salvation the consequences of sin are left intact.

Can one really call this salvation?

In Jesus Christianity, faith has quite a different object and outcome. There is a poignant awareness of sin as understood in the framework of unethical behavior. These kinds of Christians are not blind to social or physical disorder. This kind of faith declares that sin and its effects can be obliterated, and the world can be redeemed by the application of love to both the social and physical worlds. But humans must do it in the same way as Jesus did it – by redemptive love.

The proposition that love is the only way to right the wrongs of this world requires faith. It is a faith ridiculed and denounced by contemporary culture. But the faithful will press on in the face of ridicule or persecution. This kind of Christian faith declares that redemption can occur if love is the central dynamic of all relationships. This kind of Christianity rejects violence as a way to solve problems.

Although I have described Jesus' way of life as a way of faith, a particular kind of ethical faith, there may be more. Most of us have been influenced by scientific methodology and want evidence to support our faith. Jesus Christianity does find significant corroboration from scientific knowledge. Even common sense should help us.

If one wishes one's children to grow into full happy human beings capable of living to their full potential, does one apply the emotion of hate or the emotion of love? Does one practice violent control or loving care?

One could ask these same questions of every relationship in any context and the answers would be the same. But it takes a fully redeemed and developed human life to do it. It cannot be done by those trapped by a faith in either supernatural or natural violence.

How does all this relate to the world and social responsibility? Can one really be responsible for the world and one's fellowman? Can religion separate itself from the supernatural world in some way and become engaged with the real world? Can ethics and Christianity be brought together? Jesus seemed to think so.

The separation of religion and ordered behavior was a reality in some sectors of the Greek world. Customary behaviors - folkways, mores, and laws - were matters for the city fathers. Interaction with the supernatural world was the concern of religion, priests and temples. Constantinian Christianity, in its obsession with the supernatural world, perpetuated this separation of religion and ordered ethical behavior. As obligations to the supernatural world take center stage, ethical considerations recede to the background.

The Hebrew people struggled with the relationship between religion and ethics.[33] The "priestly tradition" ritualized supernatural relationships and elaborated the mechanics of worship. The "prophetic tradition" emphasized an integral relationship between the supernatural world and human social behavior. Centuries of debate and confusion continued into Jesus day.

Jesus resolved the matter to his own satisfaction and the satisfaction of many of his followers, even his followers in the 21st century. His resolution however brought consternation to both Jewish religious and Roman political authorities. Such anxiety ultimately led to their collusion in his death.

Jesus' resolution is no more popular today than it was 2,000 years ago. His call to become fully responsible human beings, with an obligation to love, is not popular with those who cling to a supernatural world and a supernaturally administered salvation. Jesus' call to social order based on peace and love is deemed impossible, irresponsible, and even reprehensible. Those committed to the violence of Calvary as the means of salvation also are committed to violence as the means to social order. They continue to denounce Jesus' resolution as foolishness.

However, those who practice faith in Jesus' way do find his way to be the way to personal and social salvation.

# THE SACRALIZATION OF VIOLENCE

Of the five events, which lie at the core of Constantinian Christianity, the crucifixion of Jesus is central.

Constantinian Christianity points to this event as the device by which life in this world and the next is determined.

The crucifixion event is a violent event. A more cruel, gruesome and terrifying way to end life is hard to imagine. It is violence at its best. It was a public violent act designed to strike terror in the hearts and minds of potential troublemakers and all observers.

It was the legal means of capital punishment and widely practiced in the Roman judicial system. Thousands of malefactors and various kinds of social disturbers were removed from society by this means. Jesus of Nazareth was only one of many thousands who were killed to free the society of sin and evil, sinners and evildoers. Three men who fit these categories were violently crucified in one day at Calvary in Palestine, a remote province of the Roman empire. How many more were crucified on that day in the whole of the empire? No one knows, or cares. Such events occurred with marvelous regularity.

For the Romans, as for every society, social order was

111

crucial. Nonconformists and violators of social order were customarily removed. In the Roman legal system it was presumed that order could be preserved only if malcontents and disturbers were sacrificed to the requirements of the law and the expectations of the system.

Death of troublemakers is the surest means to maintain order. This is the nature and purpose of capital punishment. The law of the society must be satisfied and order maintained. Life must be sacrificed if evil is to be expunged and order restored.

In our age we have something of a single-world society. In this 21st century, one hears some people talk about expunging evil from the whole world. But what is evil? Who is evil? It is a marvel how the powerful can define so exactly who and what is evil in our world!

In the religious institution, with its concern about both the natural and supernatural world, evil is a persistent and intriguing problem. If evil occurs, the supernatural world becomes disordered; the gods and their earthly representatives are displeased. In the supernatural world, as in the judicial dimensions of societies, sacrifice of life is the device to restore order. The wellbeing of supernatural and natural beings and their interaction depends on the extirpation of sin.

Violence and order, in this view of things, are inextricably connected.

In Constantinian Christianity, disorder and sin are interchangeable terms. The catalogue of sin is extensive and expands as religious functionaries and their ideological compatriots gain power. The greater this catalogue, the greater the opportunities for control. As the opportunities for control increase, the power of the powerful expands.

The formula is simple. The more evil and evildoers, the

greater the power of those who administer the solution for sin. It is always in the interests of the powerful to expand the catalogue of sin. But, interestingly and explicably, evil always encompasses the behavior of the oppressed, the disadvantaged, the alien, and anything and anybody the powerful find inconvenient.

Given the nature of power, the powerful are always right. There is never evil in the halls of power.

Jesus, with his message of love and justice questioned this arrangement of power and evil. He questioned the control by spiritual and secular authorities, as they applied violence to ordinary people. He, himself, was subsequently removed from Palestinian society by powerful religious and political authorities.

Constantinian Christianity has put an uncommon twist on this most common of events in the Roman Empire.

The violent demise of Jesus has come to be the ultimate device to deal with the problem of evil. In this creedal confessional Christian view, the crucifixion of Jesus is a sacrifice sufficient to produce universal order in the entire universe. His death, by mental manipulation activated by something called faith, has become the ultimate solution for evil. It is a device to reconcile humans with the supernatural world. It is a device to finally transport humans to the supernatural realm for eternal fraternity with the deities.

What is remarkable about this sacrifice is the interplay of the principle actors as the drama of salvation from evil is worked out in the few hours at Calvary. In this drama, the supernatural deity has been offended by the behavior of earthly beings whom he created.

Logic would dictate that he start over with a better model. The Noah story broached this possibility. The selected sample failed almost immediately.

But order really requires the elimination of the sinner. To carry out such a sentence meant the destruction of the entire human population of the earth – since all have sinned. This would have been convincing evidence that the perfect and all-powerful deity had failed in his crowning creation.

Failure by the perfect deity could never be admitted. Therefore, creedal religion concocted a scheme to eliminate the sin, but save the sinner.

The creedal God accomplishes this feat by incarnating himself as one of his creatures. He designates this creature as his son. Moreover he assigns this creature to be representative, in some way, of all mankind.

This God-man, although perfect and sinless, is forensically loaded with sin. God wills the death of his own son. God kills his own son although he uses religious and political authorities to perform the deed.

This awful, gruesome, horrendous, utterly revolting act – the crucifixion – is an adequate sacrifice to satisfy the laws of the perfectly righteous, but offended, God of the universe. This is the ultimate demonstration of a loving God! This enables humans to escape the consequences of their own sin and evil!

This act, it is claimed, restores order in the universe. This violent drama, it is affirmed, reconciles all human creatures to the powers of the supernatural world. Constantinian Christianity now declares that this was God's plan from the beginning of time.

It takes but a moment of honest and courageous thought to recognize this as a forensic drama. It is a matter of words. It is a set of mental constructs. Religious fundamentalists call this "the plan of Salvation." It is a forensic scheme completely devoid of redemptive power. Yet multitudes think and talk as though it were real. Such is the nature of Constantinian faith.

The implication of this formula is momentous.

The violence of the crucifixion is the device to deal with sin, sinners, evil and evildoers. It is the violence – in its terrifying, endless, minute-after-eternal-minute of excruciating pain that wrenches the body and sears the soul of Jesus – which accomplishes the elimination of sin and evil. In Constantinian Christianity this violence is the ultimate, wondrous, mysterious mechanism by which God deals with the problem of evil.

For the Constantinian Christian, the violence of the crucifixion is God's way of providing an escape from hell. The true believer, in the Constantinian type of Christianity, can only conclude that violence, this violence at Calvary, is the most powerful wonderful good in the universe!

But the sinner still sins. Consequently the sacrifice must be continuous. It must be remembered periodically, reenacted annually. As technology reproduces and graphically improves on the original event, the gruesome violence impacts mind and emotions with monstrous magic. Some even declare that this violence gives meaning to their lives.

Constantinian Christianity, embedded most visibly in American Christian fundamentalism, is committed to this efficacious violence. The violence of "Good" Friday is the ultimate good, for it solves the problem of ultimate evil.

Violence is thus sacralized. It is the defining act of the creedal confessional God in relation to the human race. It is God's solution to evil in this world and the supernatural world. It is a sacred act, which the devotees of God may engage in to deal with the problem of evil – as they see it –

regardless of where it occurs in the world.

It is this Godly scheme of things that inspired the Crusades, the torments of the medieval era, the Inquisition, and the horrendous persecutions of non-conformists during the Reformation. It is this divinely-inspired behavior which tortured and burned my ancestors in the 16th century.

It is the same kind of God that sacralizes violence as a solution to all human problems, whether local or far away. It is the kind of ideology that has driven the American nation for more than 200 years.

Salvation and freedom have come to be equal, if not identical, in the American mind. In this system of thought, salvation and freedom require violence. This is the American mantra; it is the American ideology. The nation was founded in the violence of war. Freedom comes as the consequence of violence. The American deity was formed in the fires of war. Devotees of American national religion and American religious fundamentalism believe their society and their religion were founded in acts of violence sponsored and blessed by God himself.

And it was. But few Americans are aware that this God is only a local, national, tribal deity. The kind of deity that takes a fearful violent approach to all tribes and nations who do not bow down to it.

In this ideological system, violence becomes the fundamental good, the foundation of freedom. The creedal God brought salvation by violence. The American God brings freedom by violence.

The fundamentalist God and the fundamentalist nation justify every war with this kind of ideology. The American God defines evil at home and abroad. This deity defines who is evil – what social structures are evil, what religious ideas are evil, what social systems are evil. Missions are designed to root out evil by the holy sacralized means of violence.

American patriots continue to think freedom comes by violence. Religious fundamentalists continue to think that violence brings salvation. The ideologies are identical, with devastating consequences to all peoples of the world.

Whose freedom? Whose salvation? What kind of freedom? What kind of salvation? Are there alternate definitions of evil? These questions are never asked in theocratic, ideologically-driven societies.

The violence that killed a million Vietnamese and 50,000 young Americans was justified by an ideology based on a particular view of the universe and a local capitalistic definition of economic evil. The economic system of communism, in American ideology, was an ultimate Godless evil. It had to be expunged by God-approved violence. With this theological view of the world, humans – even American young people – have no worth except as sacrifices for the preservation of ideological truth. They are sainted for their sacrifice. How many are killed and who is killed is immaterial. What is important is preserving the ideologically-determined truth. It makes little difference that the lying perpetrators of all wars have their own private, selfish purposes – purposes that are always antithetical to the best interests of their own populations.

And the masses of people are never swayed by the interests of humanity, but they are moved by fear and supernaturally-endorsed ideologies.

This same ideology undergirded the war that split Korea, and is leading to continuing fearsome threats in that region. It led to the initial forays into Somalia and Afghanistan and laid the groundwork for the ultimate disintegration of both those societies. It is the same ideology that led to Rumsfeld's support of Saddam Hussein in the slaughter of hundreds of thousands of Iranian youth in the early 1980s. It is the same ideology which motivated Ollie North to supply the weapons and bombs which demolished schools and rural medical clinics in Nicaragua in the early 1980s.

Evil ultimately gets defined as any activity or idea that is different than the practices, behaviors and social structures of powerful nations. None are excepted. A different form of social structure, a different set of ideas, a different culture automatically becomes evil in the fear-ridden minds of powerful ideologically-driven societies. In theological terms, God blesses the powerful and all their ways. Contrary ways are evil and must be undone at any cost.

In creedal Christian society it is God's work to destroy evil. God took care of sin by a profoundly-inexplicable supernatural act of violence at Calvary. The American deity takes care of evil by violent means all over the world. Dare any human being question the profundity of the creedal God? Dare anyone question the worldwide violence of the ideologically-driven American patriot?

For those who would follow Jesus, the teacher of love and justice, Calvary has nothing to do with human salvation. It was the scene of a violent act committed by religious and political powers who feared the power of the ethics of love, redemption and true salvation proclaimed and lived by Jesus.

The violence at Calvary is the antithesis of everything Jesus taught and practiced. Real human salvation was killed by the God of violence at Calvary. Violence provides neither salvation nor freedom on Good Friday or any other day through all of time.

# SOME ANTECEDENTS OF FIRST CENTURY NEAR EASTERN THOUGHT

Mithraism is a philosophical and religious system developed in ancient Persia. This system of thought is also known as Zoroastrianism, a credit to one of its foremost teachers. Some scholars believe the basic ideas were present as early as 2000 BCE and matured over two millennia with additions and modifications into the turn of our era.

Although the time of the emergence of specific dogmas is uncertain, there is no uncertainty about the immense impact on ancient Asian and European cultures. One of the core concepts was the principle of dualism. Everything has its opposite. A few elementary examples might introduce us to manifold possibilities: good and bad, light and dark, summer and winter, black and white, male and female, hot and cold, good and bad, gods and devils. In all cultures informed by Persian thought, the idea of duality is present in the mental constructs related to both the natural and supernatural worlds.

In northern India, the opposites present in dualism were deified; a factor accounting for the multitude of gods in Hinduism. Other normative behavioral aspects of Zoroastrianism were transplanted and ultimately revived and refurbished in Buddha's reformation in mid-millennia BCE.

In China, the dualistic idea was expanded in the system of Taoism taught by Lao Tzu. However, Taoist thought rejected the exclusive nature of absolute opposites and admitted elements of opposites in each other. Thus, if one acknowledged the existence of some truth one must also admit the truth in its opposite. In some ways, such a worldview led to a general acceptance of things as they were and an ethos of fatalism touched with optimism. Difficult times would surely lead on to better times. There was always a silver lining in every cloud.

The western version of Zoroastrianism retained the more absolute form of dualism. Ideas and behaviors were considered absolutely right or absolutely wrong. But dualism was not the only contribution to developing cultures in the Near East.

By the fourth century BCE doctrines and practices of this religion were found in Asia Minor. Although it was initially proscribed, the philosophy gradually spread among the Roman legions from the eastern reaches of the empire to the western and northern frontiers and finally, in modified forms, to Rome itself. The architectural and artistic remains of Mithraic sites are found in the Near East, particularly Asia Minor, and in Europe as far north as Hadrian's Wall in the British Isles.

As elements of Persian culture moved from region to region, they amalgamated with local cultures and transformed beliefs and practices. It impacted the religion of the Babylonians and through them influenced Arabic and early Semitic peoples.

By the turn of our era the Aramaic and Greek-speaking populations had been immersed in aspects of this culture for many centuries. By the first century CE, the Greco-Roman civilization on its frontiers and particularly Asia Minor found this system of thought remarkably dynamic.

In as much as these civilizations were the antecedents of our modern world, the early Persian ideas must also be recognized as primary antecedents of Christianity. What were these critical antecedents?

Research in the 20th century has informed scholars and lay people alike about the behavior patterns, nature of rites, the meaning of symbols, and the extensive and complicated theology of this ancient and durable system of thought.

A central God in the Persian pantheon was Mithra, a complex deity. He was the son of the supreme God Ahura-Mazda. His mother was a human virgin, Anahita. He was born in a stable. Mithra was at once both human, divine and spirit.

The most common artistic representations found in ceremonial and ritualistic sites of Mithrianism, shows him in the act of killing a bull.[34] This demonstrated Mithra's power over nature. The second most common symbol found at such sites are artistic representations of an assembly of people at a feast eating meat and drinking a potion. The potion was composed of the bull's blood, fat and Hoama juice. This rite was associated with a prayer to Mithra, "Spirit of Spirit, if it be your will, give me over to immortal birth so that I may be born again and the sacred spirit may breathe in me."[35] This ceremony, in the usual interpretation, brought renewal and immortality to devotees.

The killing of a bull and ritual washing in blood for purification persisted in the Taurobolium ceremony of first-century Greek culture in Asia Minor. In this rite, a bull was slaughtered on a lattice work of poles over a pit. Devotees of this cult knelt in the pit, lifted their faces upward and allowed the blood to flow over their body. Thus, they were symbolically purified of moral and spiritual contamination.

The sacrifice of many kinds of animals was also a common practice among temple Jews even into the time of Jesus. The temple in Jerusalem was equipped with stone gutters to permit the blood to be flushed out.

Mithra, in the Babylonian version, was associated not only with the sun God, the giver of life, but also with Venus and the signs of the zodiac related to spring, renewal and new life.

Mithraism had an extensive set of beliefs related to the supernatural world and its interrelationship with this world. There was also a complex set of rules governing customary behavior in business and all manner of social relationships.[36]

As indicated above, dualism was a central idea. Good and evil were opposites and in religious terms were incarnated in deities. Mithra was set over against the deity of darkness. Surely the ideas of heaven and hell, so prominent in later religious thought, were not far away.

The priests of Zoroastrianism were known as "Magi." Zarathustra, an early Magi, when contemplating the dark side of this dualism, proclaimed an eventual salvation from the darkness by means of a "saushyant" – a savior – who he predicted would appear at the end of time and enable good to triumph over evil.

Many other doctrines integral to Zoroastrianism later became incorporated into Judaism, Christianity and the Muslim religions. Some of these include: individual judgment, resurrection, a last judgment and life everlasting.[37]

In the Roman empire, the birthday of Mithra was celebrated on December 25. Historically this was the day in which the return of the sun was evident and the renewal of earth and life could be confirmed. This reality was celebrated not only yearly, but also weekly on the Sun-day, the first day of the week.

There are numerous other legends of Mithra's life and a belief system attributed to him.[38] Many of these, in modified form, reappeared in western religions, including Hellenistic Christianity.

Mithraism was more than a religion of rituals and relationships with the supernatural world. There was also an extensive normative system of human interrelationships. The name "Mithra" meant "contract," and a handshake was the symbol. The Vesta, the scriptures of Mithraism, describes in great detail the punishments for broken contracts. But humans also made contracts with themselves to live with responsibility and intense self-discipline. In the western evolution of Mithraism, such contracts were standard. Functionally-useful marks of membership in the secret societies of the frontier Roman Legions, where Mithraism was the guiding philosophy, included: rigid self-control, respect for authoritarian social structures, formal relationships, obedience and celibacy.

These ideas, in general, informed the life and thought of the masses of people in the Near East and the Roman empire in the early centuries of our era. This was the cultural milieu from which Christian converts came.

# BIBLIOGRAPHY

Anselm, Saint - St. Anselm's Basic Writings (Translated by S. N. Deane), The Open Court Publishing Co., 1962

- Truth, Freedom and Evil, (Translated by Hopkins and Richardson), Harper Torchbooks, 1965

Armstrong, Karen - A History of God, Ballantine Books, 1994

Borg, Marcus J. - Meeting Jesus Again for the First Time, HarperSanFransisco, 1994

- Reading the Bible Again for the First Time Harper-SanFransisco, 2001

Boyce, Mary - Zoroastrians: Their Beliefs and Practices, Routledge and Kegan Paul, London, 1979

Corbett, Julia - Religion in America, Prentice Hall, 1990

Cox, Harvey - Religion in the Secular City, Toward a Post Modern Theology, 1984

Dimont, Max I. - The Jews, God, and History, New American Library, 2003

Hofer, Eric - The True Believer: Thoughts on the Nature of Mass Movements

Goertz, Hans-Jurgin, and Snyder - The Anabaptists (Christianity and Society in the Modern World), Rutledge, 1996

Johnson Roger A. et al - Critical Issues in Modern Religion, Prentice Hall, 1990

Klassen, Walter - Anabaptism: Neither Catholic, Protestant nor Jew, Conrad Press, 1973

Mack, Burton L - The Lost Gospel, HarperSanFransisco, 1993

Newman, William N. - The Social Meanings of Religion, Rand McNally, 1974

Pagels, Elaine - Beyond Belief: The Secret Gospel of Thomas, Vintage, 2004

- The Gnostic Gospels, Vintage, 1980

Robinson, John - Honest to God, Westminster John Knox Press, 1963

Taylor, Stanley - Conceptions of Institutions and the Theory of Knowledge, Bookman Associates, New York, 1956

Vermaseren, M.J. - Mithras, The Secret God, New York, 1963

Warriner, Charles K - The Emergence of Society, The Dorsey Press, Homewood, Ill., 1970

Willer, Judith - The Social Determination of Knowledge, Prentice Hall, 1971

Yoder, John Howard - The Politics of Jesus, Patenoster Press, 1994

# FOOTNOTES AND COMMENTS

[1] Klassen, Walter - <u>Neither Protestant, Catholic nor Jew</u>

[2] Acts 11.26

[3] Richard A Batey - <u>Sepphoris the Forgotten City</u> : <u>New light on Sepphoris and the Urban World of Jesus;</u>  Baker Book House, Grand Rapids Michigan, 1991
www.webedelic.com/church/seppt.htm
See also www.usd.edu/erp/Palestine/bibliogr.htm" \l "Millar"
Note particularly the quotation - "Throughout Palestine, in the countryside and especially in the great cities of the coast and the Decapolis lived Gentiles--non-Jewish people. Some of these people traced their descent from the Greek colonists settled by Alexander and his successors. They worshiped Greek and Syrian gods in temples built in the Hellenistic style. And they lived in cities or their territories with Greek political and cultural institutions and the public structures to house them: gymnasia, theaters, hippodromes, stoas. There seems no way to establish the ethnic identity of any Gentile group in Palestine. characterized most Gentiles living in Palestine as Greco-Aramaic--and even the Jews, the only group with a clear ethnic self-definition, commonly spoke Aramaic. To call these Gentiles "Greeks" or "Syrians" falsely suggests that we actually know something about their ethnic identity"

[4] Amos 5:21-24

[5] Micah 6:8

[6] See the Old Testament prophetic materials, particularly the books of Jonah, Amos and Micah

[7] The Gospel of Thomas and other Gnostic Gospels

[8] Genesis 6:2

[9] Genesis 6:4

[10] Luke 1:35

[11] Luke 1:35

[12] Genesis 6:2

[13] http://www.touregypt.net/Osiriscu.htm

[14] See Appendix A

[15] http://essenes.net/m18.htm#taurobolium

The following quotation comes from an article - ANCIENT GREEK AND ROMAN RELIGION (Morford, M. and Lenardon, R., Classical Mythology, Longman 1998).

"Shedding the blood of a bull came to be a spectacular feature of the rite of initiation into these mysteries. It was called the Taurobolium, and the initiate stood in a pit under the bull, so that its blood poured down upon him." This baptism symbolized purification, the washing away of the old life, and resurrection to a new one; and the rebirth was further symbolized by the drinking of milk, the drink of a newborn child."

Internet address

http://www.hfac.uh.edu/mcl/classics/Orpheus/Orph_Theog.html

See also - Julia Ovidia Luna - Basic principles of Religion

Nova Roma; www.nova roma.org/religio_romana

"The gods look kindly on the scrupulous observance of religious rites which have brought our country to its peak" (Ogilvie 23).

An observation

Does God need these rituals to remain powerful? As long as functionaries perform rituals and as long as worshippers continue, the gods persist. But as these services decline, the power of the gods declines. Without services the gods effectively disappear. Given this reality we can appreciate the tremendous effort to sustain and elaborate corporate activity called "worship" or "service" in contemporary religion.

[16] http://personal.monm.edu/mgullber/reflection4.htm

[17] www.nova roma.org/religio_romana

[18] Appendix E

[19] Ibid

[20] Hebrews 9:11-15 . "But when Christ appeared a high priest of the good things to come, then through the greater and more perfect tent (not made with hands, that is not of this creation) he entered once for all into the holy place, taking not the blood of goats and calves but his own blood, thus securing an eternal redemption. For if the sprinkling of defiled persons with the blood of goats and bulls and with the ashes of an heifer sanctifies for the purification of the flesh, how much more shall the blood of Christ, who through the eternal spirit offered himself without blemish to God, purify your conscience from dead works to serve the living God" Note - Compare this passage with some of the core ideas of Mithraism referred to in Appendix E

[21] See Appendix E

[22] Acts 4:12

[23] See Appendix B

[24] In Saint Anselm's <u>Basic writings</u>, Note particularly the section called "book second" pages 239-288

[25] Ibid p 257-259

[26] See Appendix C

[27] See diagram preceding Chapter 1

[28] See appendix A

[29] An Observation - Wars to defend or promote ideologies, whether they be religious or secular ideologies, have accomplished nothing but suffering and terror throughout human history. This seems particularly evident as the capacity for mayhem and slaughter increases with our technically-proficient war machines. Wars to promote capitalism or Christianity, or to eliminate terror are no exception.

[30] See Appendix A

[31] Ibid

[32] Ibid

[33] See Chapter 2

[34] The following two quotations summarize the essential points of Mithraism as described by M.J. Vermaseren, in his book <u>Mithras, The Secret God"</u> and may be found at website http://www.borndigital.com/tarsus.htm . "The bull is associated with Venus or the Moon, and seen as a symbol of spring; another metaphor of rebirth. The key symbol, the scene most commonly represented in carvings, is Mithras straddling a bull, and holding its chin or nose, slashing its throat with a dagger and releasing the hot blood. Pits around Mithraism altars suggest that the worshippers may have also *bathed ritually* in the blood. This was followed by a meal of the bull's flesh....They believed that by eating the bull's flesh and drinking its blood they would be born again just as life itself had once been created anew from the bull's blood. It was believed that the partaking of the sacrament ensured eternal life, the immediate passing, after death, to the bosom of Mithra, there to tarry in bliss until the judgment day. On the judgment day the Mithraic keys of heaven would unlock the gates of Paradise for the reception of the faithful; whereupon all the unbaptised of the living and the dead would be annihilated upon the return of Mithra to earth. It was taught that, when a man died, he went before Mithras for judgment, and that at the end of the world Mithras would summon all the dead from their graves."

[35] Boyce, Mary P 29 "Zoroaster was thus the first to teach the doctrines

of an individual judgment, Heaven and Hell, the future resurrection of the body, the general Last Judgment, and life everlasting for the reunited soul and body. These doctrines were to become familiar articles of faith to much of mankind, through borrowings by Judaism, Christianity and Islam; yet it is in Zoroastrianism itself that they have their fullest logical coherence...."Boyce also comments on page 1 of her book, "Zoroastrianism is the oldest of the revealed world-religions, and it has probably had more influence on mankind, directly and indirectly, than any other single faith."

[36] Avesta: Vendidad: Fargard 4-12 Translated by James Darmesteter (From *Sacred Books of the East*, American Edition, 1898.)

[37] Sacrifice and resurrection are common themes among countless belief systems. Patterned by early people after the cycles of nature, their religions often centered on themes of death, rebirth and transformation. Saul (now Paul) no doubt found it easier to convert the People of Tarsus and Asia Minor by weaving the story of Jesus in with their own beliefs, and making it more palatable to them. Thus were formed the "Paulist doctrines" that form Christianity as we know it today, *i.e, God's love compelled him to sacrifice his only son, so that our sins could be forgiven, washed in the savior's blood, and the ritual eating of the flesh and drinking the blood of God, etc.*. Using the blood and sacrifice motif, Paul took Mithraism up a step, from an animal to a God-man being sacrificed; a potent and compelling idea. An idea that differs, though, from what Jesus taught, which was a Buddhist influenced, psychedelic, shamanistic oneness with God and eternity. With this new inflection of the resurrection idea, Paul went on to convert huge numbers of people, finding plentiful fodder in the Roman cities teeming with displaced war refugees, victims of the Roman conquests.

[38] Mithras, after performing his deeds, was said to have ascended to heaven in a chariot of fire, to become the intercessor for the human race among the gods on high.